TeX's 2^5 Anniversary:
A Commemorative Collection

TeX's 2^5 Anniversary: A Commemorative Collection

Editors
KARL BERRY
DAVID WALDEN

Illustrations
DUANE BIBBY

TeX Users Group
Portland, Oregon

TeX Users Group, Publishing
P.O. Box 2311
Portland, OR 97208-2311
USA

ISBN 978-0-9824626-1-4
First printing, 2010

To Donald Knuth
and his Stanford collaborators
in creating the world of TEX

Contents

Preface vii

Foreword, by Barbara Beeton ix

Part I: Donald Knuth 2

1 The current state of things 4

2 The future of TeX and METAFONT 8

3 Question & Answer Session, Oxford, 1999 12

4 The TeX tuneup of 2008 20

Part II: Early participants 31

5 David Fuchs, The format of TeX's DVI files: Version 1 34

6 John Hobby, A METAFONT-like system with PostScript output . 44

7 Frank Liang, TeX and hyphenation 56

8 Oren Patashnik, BibTeX 101 60

9 Michael Plass, Charting your grammar with TeX 68

10 Tomas Rokicki, Packed (PK) font file format 74

11 Luis Trabb Pardo, The status of the PASCAL implementation of TeX 86

12 Howard Trickey, Porting TeX to VAX/UNIX 92

Preface

Donald Knuth's dissatisfaction with the typesetting of the second edition of one of the volumes of his magnum opus *The Art of Computer Programming* and his consequent decision to develop a new computer-based typesetting system is well known. As is his practice, Professor Knuth comprehensively documented the need for better typesetting ("Mathematical Typography," reprinted as chapter 2 of *Digital Typography*, Donald Knuth, CLSI Publications, Stanford University, 1999). He has also retroactively published some of his earliest notes on the system he began developing in 1977 and first released in 1978 (*Digital Typography*, chapters 24 and 25).

As a Stanford faculty member, Prof. Knuth had students who could join in his research and share in the design and development work. Chapter 25 of *Digital Typography* mentioned above, written in 1977, already mentions turning some implementation work over to Michael Plass and Frank Liang. These students were the first in a succession of contributors at Stanford who were close to Prof. Knuth and helped in one way or another to implement key parts of TeX.

With this annual TUG conference in San Francisco celebrating the 2^5 (thirty-second) anniversary of TeX, Prof. Knuth and other Stanford TeX developers were invited to participate in the conference, and kindly accepted. We tried to think of a suitable gesture with which to honor them, and the creation of this commemorative volume of reprints from *TUGboat* seemed most appropriate.

To set the context, we invited one other person who has been in the TeX world since nearly the beginning to contribute a foreword: Barbara Beeton, from the American Mathematical Society.

As listed in the preceding table of contents, we have included three papers by Prof. Knuth, one Q&A session with him, and one paper each from eight of his collaborators. Knuth's papers are Part 1 of this volume. The other contributors' papers make up Part 2, which is ordered alphabetically by the authors' last names.

The approximate chronological order of the papers is as follows, with our chapter number listed at the beginning of the line:

11.	Zabala & Trabb Pardo on the PASCAL implementation status	October 1980
5.	Fuchs on DVI format	July 1981
7.	Liang on TeX and hyphenation	July 1981
9.	Plass on applying TeX to grammar charts	November 1981
1.	Knuth on (then) current and future plans for TeX	October 1981
12.	Trickey & Curtis on porting TeX to VAX/UNIX	April 1983
10.	Rokicki on PK packed file format	November 1985
8.	Patashnik on BibTeX	June 1998
6.	Hobby on MetaPost	December 1989
2.	Knuth on completing his TeX/METAFONT work	November 1990
3.	Knuth question & answer session in Oxford	September 1999
4.	Knuth on his most recent TeX/METAFONT tuneup	May 2008

We mostly preserved formatting details, instead of trying to unify all these disparate sources produced over a three-decade time span. The main difference from the originals is the line length of this book (compared to *TUGboat*), and general usage of the current Computer Modern fonts. We have not given the authors any opportunity to correct anything they might now like to change or correct in the papers.

Finally, we have scattered images created over the years by Duane Bibby throughout the book. Duane also created a new image for the front cover. The very last drawing in the book, accompanying the article by Howard Trickey, was also created for the book — a late-breaking bonus to try to make up for our unwitting omission of Howard from the cover drawing.

Thanks to Barbara Beeton not only for her gracious foreword, but also for her superlative editing skills (as always); to Hans Hagen for supplying more Bibby drawings at the last minute; to the Computer Science Department at the University of Aarhus in Denmark, which supports the main TUG server, where we developed this book; and to Robin Laakso, TUG's executive director, who organized the TUG 2010 conference and supported us in many ways during the creation of this book.

Karl Berry & David Walden
April 2010

There is some confusion about what is a preface, a foreword, and an introduction. The terms are often interchanged without any apparent reason.

— Marshall Lee, *Bookmaking: The Illustrated Guide to Design and Production* (1965)

Foreword
Barbara Beeton

Thoughts on TeX at 2^5

Who would have thought that we'd still be here, publishing articles about using TeX after 32 years! It's been an interesting journey.

I was sent to Stanford in the summer of 1979 to learn TeX while the TeX project was in full swing. Don Knuth introduced me to the members of the project, and assigned David Fuchs to watch over me. The first thing that DRF did was sit me down in front of a small green-screened monitor, launched the Emacs tutorial, and said "learn it." Learn it I did; it has been a dependable tool through all these years.

The green screen was the window into SAIL — both the DECsystem-10 at the Stanford Artificial Intelligence Lab and the eponymous programming language in which TeX was first written. Scattered through the building were various exotic output devices — an XGP (Xerox Graphics Printer) and several Versatec electrostatic printers. The XGP was about the size of a refrigerator, and used ordinary letter-size paper; it used a much coarser grade of toner than we're now used to, and occasionally hiccupped, leaving granules of carbon along with the print on the output page. The Versatec was roll-fed with coated paper; little metal fingers put rows of charges on the paper, which then went through an oppositely-charged solvent bath that deposited a gray image on the paper. Both of these devices had a resolution of 200 dpi, so the convention was to set the output at a magnification of 130 percent that was then reduced photographically to the intended size.

TeX had a rather different syntax in the beginning from what we're used to now, but it was even then obvious that the best approach was to identify the structure of a target document and devise an appropriate user interface. The raw primitives could always be used in an emergency, but it was better (it still is) to avoid the need.

Don was generous with his time and assistance. I had brought a number of "real world" problems that had actually been encountered in the production of existing publications. One of my favorites was the execrable column break that occurred in a city heading in the middle of the geographic listing of one year's Combined Membership List, shown to the right. Making that element into an unbreakable unit, and one that also wouldn't be separated from the listing of names that followed, gave me a real sense of accomplishment. Other examples of elements used in AMS administrative publications appear in Appendix D (Dirty Tricks) of *The TeXbook*; these are a lasting reminder of Don's careful attention to the needs of other users besides himself.

The crew from AMS that spent July 1979 at Stanford have now mostly moved on, but their influence lingers. Mike Spivak's AMS-TeX is still preferred by a number of older mathematicians who write articles and books to be published by the AMS, and the structures defined in that work are still alive and well in AMS-LaTeX, which became part of the "required" component of LaTeX in the late 1990s. Bob Morris (who originally signed on to create the AMS-TeX macros) passed on knowledge of TeX and digital typography to his student at UMass Boston, Karl Berry, who is now the TUG president.

A year later, in March 1980, I returned to Stanford to learn how to program METAFONT and to create a prototype Cyrillic font for use in *Math Reviews.* One of the highlights of this trip was a mini-conference organized by John Seybold; this was attended by representatives of several organizations interested in math typesetting software. That's where I first met Chuck Bigelow (Chuck was then on the faculty of the Rhode Island School of Design; he now occupies the chair at Rochester Institute of Technology formerly held by Hermann Zapf). Don gave a talk about TeX and METAFONT, and after one of the demonstrations, several of the participants experimented with METAFONT to produce a new glyph, the "Knu", in honor of Don. Sadly, I no longer have the output of this experiment.

I visited Stanford to learn from the TeX project on several other occasions, and TUG meetings were held on the Stanford campus every summer until the project wound down. Much of the TUG history from this period is recorded in early issues of *TUGboat.* I treasure my memories from that period — it was a truly exciting time.

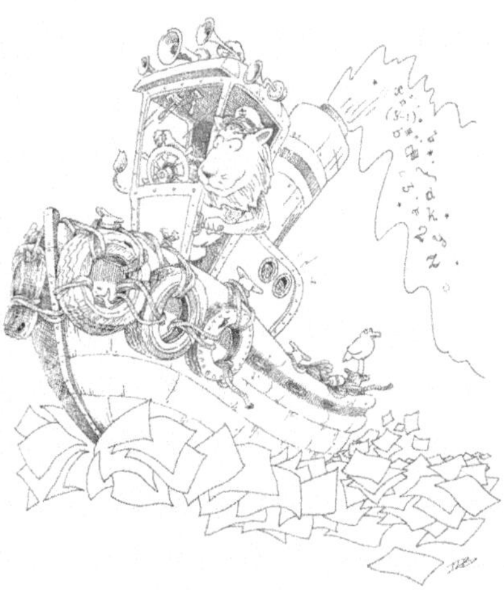

Many women have been leaders on the TeX user side
starting with Barbara Beeton,
who has been the heart of the enterprise
since the beginning.
— KARL BERRY, *Email* (2004)

My involvement with TUGboat came about around 1990
when I was drafted by Barbara Beeton,
eh, I mean: barbara beeton.
— VICTOR EIJKHOUT, *TUG Interview* (2005)

FREEWARE
FONTS
Macros
USER GROUPS
TEXLIVE
CTAN
TE
META
DK

Part I
Donald Knuth

It is a cliche to say "He needs no introduction", but it is nevertheless true when we are speaking of Donald Knuth in a book addressed to the TEX community.

We have chosen four items from Professor Knuth's many publications in *TUGboat*: (1) his 1981 announcement of the impending "definitive" release of TEX, four years after he began system design in 1977; (2) his 1990 announcement that he was done working on TEX except for periodically fixing "extremely serious bugs"; (3) a Q&A session held in Oxford in 1999; (4) his report on his 2008 tuneup of TEX.

In some sense, these papers summarize Professor Knuth's attitude toward TEX over the past 32 years. They also sketch the history of what to our knowledge is the longest running free software/open source development story and Professor Knuth's approach to making that possible. The Q&A illustrates Knuth's commitment to not only doing extraordinary work but explaining it, in his own inimitable style. Finally, the last paper shows that even when merely doing a tuneup Professor Knuth never departs from his enthusiastic and precise approach to the art of computer programming and analysis of algorithms.

Bibliographic information on Professor Knuth is also available from other sources: a list of interviews of him at `http://tug.org/interviews`, his introductions in his seven collections of papers in different areas of his research, and fan web sites dedicated to him.

TUGboat bibliography

The current state of things [**2**:3, November 1981]

Fixed-point glue setting — an example of WEB [**3**:1, March 1982]

A note on hyphenation [**4**:2, September 1983]

Observations on TEX from a divergent viewpoint: Comments, response, and reresponse [**4**:2, September 1983]

TEX incunabula [**5**:1, May 1984]

Comments on quality in publishing [**5**:1, May 1984]

A course on METAFONT programming [**5**:2, November 1984]

Recipes and fractions [**6**:1, March 1985]

Remarks to celebrate the publication of *Computers & Typesetting* [**7**:2, June 1986]

The TEX logo in various fonts [**7**:2, June 1986]

It happened: Announcement of TEX 2.1 [**8**:1, April 1987]

Mixing right-to-left texts with left-to-right texts (with Pierre MacKay) [**8**:1, April 1987]

Problem for a Saturday afternoon [**8**:1, April 1987]

Fonts for digital halftones [**8**:2, July 1987]

Macros for Jill [**8**:3, November 1987]

A punk Meta-Font [**9**:2, August 1988]

TEX would find it difficult ... [**10**:1, April 1989]

Typesetting *Concrete Mathematics* [**10**:1, April 1989]

The new versions of TEX and METAFONT [**10**:3, November 1989]

Notes on the errors of TEX [**10**:4, December 1989]

Virtual fonts: More fun for Grand Wizards [**11**:1, April 1990]

Exercises for *TEX: The Program* [**11**:2, June 1990]

The future of TEX and METAFONT [**11**:4, December 1990]

Arthur Lee Samuel, 1901–1990 [**11**:4, December 1990]

Answers to Exercises for *TEX: The Program* [**11**:4, December 1990]

Fixed-point glue setting: Errata [**12**:2, June 1991]

An interview with Donald Knuth, November 1991 [**13**:4, December 1992]

Icons for TEX and METAFONT [**14**:4, December 1993]

TUG'95: Questions and answers with Prof. Donald E. Knuth [**17**:1, March 1996]

Important message regarding CM fonts [**17**:1, March 1996]

Amsterdam, 13 March 1996 — Knuth meets NTG members [**17**:4, December 1996]

CSTUG, Charles University, Prague, March 1996 — Questions and answers with Prof. Donald E. Knuth [**17**:4, December 1996]

Interview: Donald E. Knuth [**21**:2, June 2000]

Question & Answer session with Donald Knuth, UK-TUG, Oxford, Sunday, 12 September 1999 [**22**:1-2, March/June 2001]

Donald Knuth: All questions answered (University of Oslo, 30 August 2002) [**23**:3-4, 2002]

Interview with Donald E. Knuth [**26**:3, 2005]

TEX's infinite glue is projective [**28**:1, 2007]

The TEX tuneup of 2008 [**29**:2, 2008]

... the designer of a new system
must not only be the implementor and first large-scale user:
the designer should also write the first user manual.

— DONALD KNUTH, *Software — Practice and Experience* (1989)

1

The current state of things

[Published in *TUGboat* **2**:3, November 1981]

STANFORD UNIVERSITY
STANFORD, CALIFORNIA 94305-2085

DONALD E. KNUTH
Fletcher Jones Professor
Department of Computer Science

Telephone:
(416) 497-4367

October 13, 1981

To: Coordinators of TEX implementations
From: Donald Knuth
Subject: Current state of things

For some reason I woke up this morning with the feeling that some of you were wondering what I have been up to recently. So I decided to write a short note about present and future plans for TEX.

I'm going to be releasing the "definitive" TEX early next year. The manual will be rewritten, and all the code will also be rewritten, although of course the existing manual and program will be pretty close to the finished product. A hardcover book will be published containing both the manual and the complete program documentation. The manual by itself will also be published separately in paperback.

Naturally I want to make sure that no bugs are present in either the manual or the system, so I will be distributing numerous preprints of all the material for comments and testing, until a high level of confidence has been reached.

The present implementations of TEX in SAIL and in PASCAL seem to be quite stable. With thousands of users, many of whom are quite sophisticated, no bugs have been reported for several months. The new implementation will make the present ones obsolete, of course, but we are still distributing copies of the current implementations to new users.

At the moment I am completing the development of a new documentation system called `WEB`. This is a greatly improved version of the 1979 `DOC/UNDOC/TEXDOC` system used for the first implementation of TEX in PASCAL; the new names are `WEB/TANGLE/WEAVE`. Basically, the `WEB` language describes a program's structure, using a mixture of TEX and PASCAL that can be considered as an extension of both languages to do much more than either language can do separately. The `TANGLE` program inputs a `WEB` description and rearranges everything so that a syntactically correct PASCAL program is obtained as output. The `WEAVE` program combines the TEX and PASCAL portions of `WEB` description with TEX formatting macros, so that the resulting TEX file will generate a structured documentation.

The "definitive" TEX, which will be officially known as `TEX82`, will of course be defined as a web. At present I'm finished with the "hardest" 20 per cent of this revision. There will be no "SYSDEP" module as in the present implementation; the system dependent parts will, however, be much simpler than they are now and their TEX-specific features will be moved to system-independent parts of the implementation.

The best way to speed up the process of `TEX82` installation seems to be to prepare for it in advance, by installing the `WEB` system. Therefore I plan to distribute preliminary copies of the following in mid-November:

(1) WEB User Manual (hardcopy)

(2) WEAVE.WEB (the WEAVE program, in WEB language)

(3) TANGLE.WEB (the TANGLE program, in WEB language)

(4) TANGLE.PAS (the PASCAL program that TANGLE outputs when you apply it to itself)

(5) WEBHDR.TEX (macros used to print the output of WEAVE)

You need (4) for bootstrapping, after which you can change TANGLE and WEAVE as needed for your system. A few system-dependent subroutines are present in TANGLE and WEAVE, but the necessary changes are trivial compared to those in the existing TEX, so I doubt if it will take long to install this system.

(The bootstrapping process is a little interesting: First you change the system-dependent parts of TANGLE.PAS and TANGLE.WEB, until you can get TANGLE to reproduce itself. Then you make the same changes to the system-dependent parts of WEAVE.WEB. Then you can use TANGLE to create a working program WEAVE.PAS. Then you can use WEAVE to create the files WEAVE.TEX and TANGLE.TEX, from which the compiler that you now have will generate beautiful documentation listing. Next year when you get TEX.WEB, your job will be to make similar changes to its system-dependent parts, after which WEAVE and TANGLE will produce the TEX.TEX and TEX.PAS files you need to get TEX82 going.)

Our preliminary experiments with software generation using WEB have proved to be quite successful, so you may in fact get some use out of this before TEX82 arrives. Of course, the WEB system will only be a few weeks old in mid-November, so you will also be able to help us diagnose any bugs that it may contain, if you arc interested.

I hope to have TEX.WEB ready for testing by the end of this year and to have a draft of the new manual done by the end of January. After TEX is finished, the same will be done for METAFONT, but that will take some time.

Now I have a question for you: Do you want to be one of the guinea pigs who receive the first WEB system in November? If so, please send a letter as soon as possible to Dr. Arthur Samuel, Dept. of Computer Science, Stanford University, Stanford CA 94305, telling (a) where to send the material, (b) if you can get it over the ARPANET or if a tape should be sent. And please enclose $25.00 if you can, since that will defray our expenses of making and sending the tape.

DEK/pw

I guess I must have ink in my veins:
When I first learned about the potential of digital printing technology,
I couldn't resist putting the rest of my life on hold
while I tried to adapt the typographical wisdom of previous centuries
to the possibilities of the present day.

— DONALD KNUTH, *Digital Typography* (1999)

2

The future of TeX and METAFONT

[Published in *TUGboat* **11**:4, November 1990]

My work on developing TEX, METAFONT, and Computer Modern has come to an end. I will make no further changes except to correct extremely serious bugs.

I have put these systems into the public domain so that people everywhere can use the ideas freely if they wish. I have also spent thousands of hours trying to ensure that the systems produce essentially identical results on all computers. I strongly believe that an unchanging system has great value, even though it is axiomatic that any complex system can be improved. Therefore I believe that it is unwise to make further "improvements" to the systems called TEX and METAFONT. Let us regard these systems as fixed points, which should give the same results 100 years from now that they produce today.

The current version number for TEX is 3.1, and for METAFONT it is 2.7. If corrections are necessary, the next versions of TEX will be 3.14, then 3.141, then 3.1415, ..., converging to the ratio of a circle's circumference to its diameter; for METAFONT the sequence will be 2.71, 2.718, ..., converging to the base of natural logarithms. I intend to be fully responsible for all changes to these systems for the rest of my life. I will periodically study reports of apparent bugs, and I will decide whether changes need to be made. Rewards will be paid to the first finders of any true bugs, at my discretion, but I can no longer afford to double the size of the reward each year. Whenever I have created a new version, I will put it in the official master TEX archive, which currently resides at Stanford University. At the time of my death, it is my intention that the then-current versions of TEX and METAFONT be forever left unchanged, except that the final version numbers to be reported in the "banner" lines of the programs should become

```
TeX, Version $\pi$
```

and

```
METAFONT, Version $e$
```

respectively. From that moment on, all "bugs" will be permanent "features."

As stated on the copyright pages of Volumes B, D, and E, anybody can make use of my programs in whatever way they wish, as long as they do not use the names TEX, METAFONT, or Computer Modern. In particular, any person or group who wants to produce a program superior to mine is free to do so. However, nobody is allowed to call a system TEX or METAFONT unless that system conforms 100% to my own programs. as I have specified in the manuals for the TRIP and TRAP tests. And nobody is allowed to use the names of the Computer Modern fonts in Volume E for any fonts that do not produce identical `tfm` files. This prohibition applies to all people or machines, whether appointed by TUG or by any other organization. I do not intend to delegate the responsibility for maintenance of TEX, METAFONT, or Computer Modern to anybody else, ever.

Of course I do not claim to have found the best solution to every problem. I simply claim that it is a great advantage to have a fixed point as a building block. Improved macro packages can be added on the input side; improved device drivers can be added on the output side. I welcome continued research that will lead to alternative systems that can typeset documents better than TEX is able to do. But the authors of such systems must think of another name.

That is all I ask, after devoting a substantial portion of my life to the creation of these systems and making them available to everybody in the world. I sincerely hope that the members of TUG will help me to enforce these wishes, by putting severe pressure on any person or group who produces any incompatible system and calls it

TEX or METAFONT or Computer Modern — no matter how slight the incompatibility might seem.

Donald E. Knuth
Department of Computer Science
Stanford University
Stanford, CA 94305

Should TEX be extended, and in what way?
I often wish that TEX could give me more information
about the state it's in. We can use a few more features as well,
but not all wishes fit well into the way TEX operates.
. . . whenever I look into this,
I realize that Don Knuth stopped putting more features in TEX
at the moment when the solution space became too fuzzy.
— HANS HAGEN, *TUG interview* (2002)

TEX
USERS
TUG
95
FLORIDA

3

Question & Answer Session, Oxford, 1999

[Published in *TUGboat* **22**:1–2, March/June 2001]

[This Q&A session took place on 12 September 1999 in Oxford, U.K., hosted by UK-TUG on the occasion of their tenth anniversary.]

Philip Taylor: I'm sure everybody here by now knows Don Knuth. Don has very kindly agreed to do a question and answer session this evening. In order to record both the questions and the answers, we have two microphones. One for Don's use and a radio microphone so we can capture your question on the tape, as well as the answer. Many thanks. Thanks Don.

Donald Knuth (DEK): O.K., I hope you can hear me.

Audience: Use the microphone.

DEK: No, I can't use the microphone, it doesn't work for me. It's only for the tape, but I will try to project. Since I have been retired for a few years and my voice isn't what it used to be, I'll do my best.

A part of the rules are that when you ask me a question, you give your name first. Another rule is that I get to ask questions too. Occasionally.

I did prepare one small thing, because, as coming to Oxford I re-read one of my favourite novels, a Dorothy L. Sayers mystery called *Gaudy Night*, which is all about Oxford. I wanted to read you just part of it, which has to do with typesetting. [*Laughter*] In Chapter 3 it mentions a Miss Lydgate, who had prepared her magnum opus, about — I don't know how to pronounce it — prosody, the study of meters in poetry. It said her handwriting was difficult to read, her experience in dealings with printers was limited but she had invented a novel and complicated system of notation that involved the use of twelve different varieties of type; and then she had all kinds of sheets in page proofs and so on. And she said 'Don't prick your fingers on that bit of manuscript that's pinned on, I'm afraid it's rather full of marginal balloons and interlineations, but I suddenly realised I could work out a big improvement in my notation, so I've had to alter it all the way through.' Then Harriet said comfortingly, 'Well, the Oxford University Press is no doubt accustomed to deciphering the manuscripts of scholars.' [*Laughter*] Now this work of Miss Lydgate appears to play a kind of minor role in the entire book and I have a question for you here, because it said her system of scansion required five alphabets with a series of pothooks for its expression, and this is a term I don't know. What are pothooks? If any of you can tell me ...

Audience: Spell it out.

DEK: It's spelt like pot hooks, P-O-T-H-O-O-K-S.

Audience: Pothooks are hooks for hanging pots.

Male Voice: Yeah, but in typography it's an 'S' like an 'S'.

DEK: Is it some kind of special symbol? O.K. So she had these twelve fonts plus pothooks, which she used to typeset. So anyway you have some idea. Does this mike actually magnify? Can you hear me a little better? O.K. Well hello. I was reading from one of my favourite books..., but that's enough. I have one more thing prepared then I will go for questions. This was for Phil, I wanted to show you.

Thanks are due to the following:
Philip Taylor, for tape recording the Q&A session;
Jonathan Fine, for managing the transcription;
Pam George, transcribing from tape and making corrections;
Don Knuth, for diligently and promptly correcting proofs.

Laughter & Clapping: (Don shows he's wearing a T-shirt under his shirt that celebrates the Aston UK TEX Archive, 'oldest and best'.)

DEK: I always try to wear the appropriate T-shirt for the day. O.K., your turn now.

Dave Pawson: My name is Dave Pawson and I have an answer to your question. I was brought up in the 1940s and 50s in the north of England and one of the houses that I moved into was built in the mid-18th century, and around the coal burning stove and above it and beneath the mantelpiece there were a number of hooks and they were the 'pothooks' for hanging the pots on. [*The OED discusses this usage.*] Does that answer your question?

DEK: O.K. So this must be a similar shape that you would use for the symbols. I think that someone said that shorthand uses pothooks — some systems of shorthand. Thank you.

Dave Pawson: I think it's what you get when you type a left angle bracket into TEX and you are expecting a straight translation, and one of your assumptions in the big blue book comes unstuck, because it comes out like a pothook. [*Laughter*] Is that true?

DEK: Might be. The other thing I wanted to say is thank you very much to Phil Taylor for arranging that we could have the 10th anniversary celebration during the brief window of time that I could be in the U.K. I don't get to travel very often, and so now I get to remember not only the 10th anniversary celebration of TEX Users Group in America but also the one from here. At the 10th celebration in America we had the president of TUG dressed as *META* the Lion — that was Bart Childs — and now here we have Mrs. TEX as well so now my delight is complete.

Sebastian Rahtz: On your recommendation last year I bought a copy of *Life: A User's Manual* by Georges Perec, which I am still trying to read. I wonder while I'm still trying to read it whether you would like to recommend a film or a piece of music which has equal meaning to you as Georges Perec's book.

DEK: I guess when I made my home pages, a few years ago, one of the pages listed books that I was recommending to read. There's this incredibly different book by Georges Perec called *Life: A User's Manual*, which is a combination of many different kinds of artistry. It has a mathematical basis, but still becomes, I think, a great work of fiction. He developed this book with 99 chapters. (There should really be 100 chapters, but each chapter was based on a lot of mathematical constraints and one of his rules was that you had to break one of the rules, so naturally it has only 99 chapters instead.) It is the story of the people who live in an apartment block in Paris. There are 10 floors and 10 apartments on each floor, and you go through the apartments — actually some of the apartments have several rooms — but you go through the apartments in the order of a knight's tour. Eventually you find out about the lives of all these people, and there are many other very interesting constraints that he put into the book. Each chapter is a little short story, kind of independent of the others. Now you are asking if there's something else analogous, in the domain of music or ...

Sebastian Rahtz: Film.

DEK: ... or film. O.K. The closest thing in film is this new movie *Run Lola Run*, from Germany. If you were to do it the way Perec did it you would have many more chapters, but *Run Lola Run* gives you a story three times. The first time ends in disaster and so Lola says 'No take me back. Let's do it again.' So we start over and she does something slightly different in the first scene and then we go through the whole story again, but everything happens five seconds later, so certain accidents don't occur in the streets and the whole plot changes. At the end of the second telling of the story it's another disaster, not for her, but for her boyfriend, and that's too terrible to accept. The third version of the story leads to a happier fate.

In music I suppose I think of a theme that had been proposed to Bach, I think by one of the noblemen of his time. He supposedly improvised a theme on that melody spontaneously, but then he was fascinated by it afterwards. During the last year of his life he prepared a manuscript that he left unfinished at his death, called the *Art of the Fugue*. That work is analogous to Perec's, because the idea is to make a thing of beauty while working within tight constraints.

Sebastian Rahtz: Good, thank you. [*Pause*]

DEK: Well, if there are no more questions ...
[*Laughter*]

Elizabeth Gilliart: What are you going to write next?

DEK: Yes, I tend to be writing about a page a day and so there's nobody alive that has read everything I've written, except perhaps me. But I'm just finishing now a book that is incredibly specialised. It will be in the Springer Lecture Series, Lecture Notes on Computer Science, and it's called *MMIXware*. It's a set of computer programs to simulate the new RISC computer that I designed this year. MMIX is a computer for the new millennium. The first 'M' is for millennium and it replaces a computer called MIX that I used in my books on computer programming. I had the privilege of working with the designer of the DEC Alpha chip, Dick Sites, who is one of my students; John Hennessy, the designer of the MIPS chip, also was a participant in this design, and a few other people in Silicon Valley. We came up with something I think would be a fairly good machine to build in about ten years. It tries to be the cleanest computer design, and easy to learn, fairly nice to look at, and to make theories about; there is a group of people that are helping me use this new computer to rewrite the algorithms that I had written for the old computer. *MMIXware* is a set of software programs that make MMIX live even though it hasn't been built yet. The exciting thing to me is the pipeline simulator, which is a meta simulator — which means that it can simulate millions and millions of different kinds of possible implementations, or even implementations that nobody knows how to build. You can say for instance how much memory it has, what kind of caches it has, what kind of strategies the caches use to remember the recent information; a pipelined computer has different functional units, you can say how many multipliers you have and you can define a functional unit to handle any subset of the 256 operation codes; you can have any number of functional units, you can issue any number of instructions simultaneously, you can look ahead different ways and control all kinds of things. And then you can find out how fast your programs run. Now if we had that machine we could put TeX onto MMIX and see how fast it works with different kinds of caches. This program for the meta simulator is probably the most difficult computer program I ever wrote.

To me it was most interesting because it depends on the idea of literate programming that I used when I worked on TeX; for me perhaps the greatest spin-off of TeX was this idea of literate programming, which has helped me write computer programs of all kinds. I don't think I could ever have written the MMIX meta simulator without literate programming; it would have been too mind boggling. I would not have been able to get the whole thing together and debug it; it would have been too much of a mental strain, overburdening my head. In the past, literate programming has often helped me write better programs, but here for the first time it was crucial, or I couldn't have written the program at all. I don't think *MMIXware* would have been possible without a good documentation language to help me understand what I was doing as I went along. So this will be a book about 400–500 pages, but it's mostly just the typeset version of these literate programs for that new computer.

Then also I'll be finishing a sort of sequel to *Digital Typography*. *Digital Typography* is volume three of a set of collected papers; all the scientific papers that I've written are being divided into eight categories. The first book contained the things I wrote about *Literate Programming*. The second book was called *Selected Papers on Computer Science*; those were the papers I wrote for audiences that weren't primarily computer scientists; it collects the general works. And then the third volume was *Digital Typography*, and I told Phil I'd come here tonight because I'll do anything to sell copies of that book. The fourth volume will be called *Selected Papers on Analysis of Algorithms*, and those are my mathematical papers for what I think is my main unique life's work — the study of computer methods in a quantitative way: How good are particular computer methods, from a definite exact mathematical point of view? That book is estimated to be about 750 pages, and it will contain, I think 37, 38 papers on that subject. The material has all been scanned and put into TeX form. But I have to spend a few months in spare moments going through dotting the i's and crossing the t's and making the index, putting the bibliographies in a consistent format, finding out people's middle names for the index, things like that. And I also go through every paper and put it into the form in which I would like it to be remembered. So if a paper was written in the 70s and I used sexist pronouns, I change that; I try to rework it so that instead of saying 'he did it', I'll say 'they did it' or something. Also I change 'which' to 'that' a lot. It's an American thing.

Male Voice: Why?

DEK: It's actually because of an Englishman named Fowler who wrote *The King's English* and gave rules for 'which' versus 'that'. The people in America believed him and they started teaching English classes, and it was taken over then by the *New Yorker* and other well-edited journals until finally the copy editors who used Fowler's rules — Fowler's book came out in the 20s I think[1] — the copy editors who used Fowler's . . .

Audience: Roberts' rules!

DEK: Whose rules?

Audience: Just after Roberts' rules!

DEK: I never heard of Roberts' rules of English, only *Roberts' Rules of Order*[2] — and I think your comment is out of order. Anyway, Fowler essentially gave an algorithm that pretty much boils down to this: Look at what comes before the word 'which'. If it's a preposition or a comma, then it's fine; 'which' can also be a pronoun. But otherwise you change it to 'that'. Well, it got to the point where almost all of the magazines in America and most of the newspapers by the end of the 70s were using

[1]H. W. Fowler, *The King's English* (Oxford 1907). H. W. Fowler, *A Dictionary of Modern English Usage* (Oxford 1924).

[2]Somebody named Paul Roberts wrote *Understanding Grammar* in 1954, but I don't think it was terrifically influential.

'which' versus 'that' in Fowler's recommended style. This was because the copy editors had risen through the ranks and won the battle. I had written the first draft of *The TEXbook* in the old way; but Guy Steele who was visiting Stanford from MIT, marked it all up, everywhere I had a wicked 'which'. Simultaneously my copy editor from Addison-Wesley was revising volume 2 of *The Art of Computer Programing*, which I had in TEX form before the 2nd edition came out. I was doing the typesetting in 1979 and 80, and that copy editor was also a member of this new generation. So that's when I learned the algorithm for wicked 'whiches'; I could do a search with a text editor, checking to see if it's following a preposition or a comma.

Soon I became very sensitive to this, as were a lot of Americans. I started to be irritated when people would quote a sentence from my earlier papers where I used a wicked 'which'. It was even hard for me to read the New English Bible because I would silently have to translate 'which' to 'that'. I go into more detail in my book *Mathematical Writing*, published by the Math Association of America. The British perspective I understand is different still, but in America it's very much a stylistic lapse that calls attention to itself if you don't follow the convention. You can go through now say 100% of the magazines in the last 10 or 15 years and you very rarely see a wicked 'which'.

James Foster: You said that the MMIXware book was for Springer; did they ask you to use their LATEX 2.09 style files? [*Laughter*]

DEK: I take it that LATEX 2.09 style files are a joke because that's an old version of LATEX?

James Foster: We had to use them recently.

DEK: I was given a free hand here. But I'm supplying camera copy so we'll see what they say. This is the output of my own program called CTWILL, which is a special version of CWEAVE that makes little indexes on the right-hand page. One of the chapters in *Digital Typography* talks about this: 'Mini-Indexes for Literate Programs' is the title of that chapter. Basically when you are reading a computer program every name of a variable on the page that you are reading is either defined on that page or you can find it in the mini-index. And the mini-index will tell you that the variable is, say, defined in section 5, and it is a procedure name or a constant and so on. It gives you a quick reference. It's an idea that I picked up from some textbooks on languages, where people would be learning French or Russian. Given a short story in some other language, every word in the vocabulary that you might have to look up in a dictionary appears in an index on that page. With CTWILL I have a bunch of macros that check the uses and definitions of everything on a page. The macros automatically prepare mini-indexes; there is a separate pass to sort the words, but the first pass does the layout. Some of the more difficult — probably the most difficult — TEX macros that I ever wrote are involved in that. I call this program TWILL because it's sort of a double WEAVE. Anyway the CTWILL program gives me the output that I have to send to Springer.

So no, I won't be using their style files. I did one other book in their series but that was some years ago, before they had learnt to insist on those things I suppose. For some purposes of course these extra format restrictions are not only for your creativity but also for electronic archiving. It's not the kind of restrictions that Perec would have added, but I imagine the publisher sees that it's to their advantage to have as many things in that style as possible. It depends on what you are doing, because that can also stifle what you want to say. One of the things uppermost in my mind from the beginning of TeX was that I would have the freedom to introduce a new notation if it was the right thing for the subject I was writing about. If I wanted to make up a new notation I wouldn't have to go through any middlemen who wouldn't understand the notation. I would be able to typeset it and I would know that it was getting through in the way I wanted it.

Philip Taylor: I have some bad news: They really do want us out of here by half past ten, so there's time for just a couple more questions.

Jonathan Fine: I hope it's not too late to ask this question. Why did you introduce category codes?

DEK: Well, if you look at this book *Digital Typography* it shows the original draft of TeX that I made the first night when I stayed up late typing a proposed design. The feature was even more awful in those days, it handled not only category codes but all kinds of penalty amounts and other parameters; anything that I didn't know how to fix as a constant in TeX I just left for later, so that I could change it. But you know originally I didn't think of having many users; TeX was a system for me and my secretary, so I wasn't thinking of things in much generality. So the same mechanism that I had originally for category codes was also used for things like how many characters before breaking for a hyphen, what was the penalty for widows, et cetera, all done with the same mechanism 'chpar'. C-H-P-A-R it was called: Change Parameter. I had no idea of generality in the first place.

Then later on, as I saw the applications Math Reviews were making, I realized that I'd better have some way to allow more flexibility... Jonathan, you'd be interested to know that the very first implementation of proto TeX was done without recognizing control sequences as words; each character was read in as a character by itself and then the 'hash table' lookup would go on afterwards. The first implementation, which was done by my students in the summer of 77 while I was in China, was very much like Active TeX in that sense. We found out that we could make the program run a lot faster in its inner loop if we distinguished control sequences from ordinary text, but originally every character was active in the very first draft. In this book *Digital Typography* I resurrected the computer files that I had used when first getting my thoughts in order.

Dominik Wujastyk: Don, you made a change in TeX when you made it able to read an eight-bit character, and that was very important for European users and others. I completely respect and like the idea that TeX is fixed, that you've finished with it as it were for the moment, and that it is a fixed point and it's not going to change anymore. However it does look as if TeX will have to go Unicode. There is of course Omega already; I've never used Omega, I haven't had the courage to take it on yet, but I think it's there in my future, and of course other people are using it. I just wonder about whether it's going to just always be Omega or something like it and TeX, and they're just going to become separate things and go their own ways; or could you give a Unicode version of TeX some imprimatur or some special blessing, so that it becomes the one that everyone uses. I wonder whether all the development efforts can somehow be brought together again.

DEK: Yeah! It seems so difficult. I'm a great fan of Unicode, but I also know enough about it to know that it's incredibly complicated, and that I would never have a system based on Unicode that I would be able to say has no bugs in it because of the extra complexity. Well, I like TeX, I like having a program that is, if not 100%

reliable, it's 99.9999 — it's as reliable as anything. So solid that we can build on it. This means however that I'm not supporting all of the important languages that Unicode supports. Still the job of doing all of those in one system is so incredibly hard that I don't know where the expertise is going to come from to get it to such a well debugged level. For me to put my imprimatur on something would require so much work, I would have to check that the thing had been done right, and there is so much involved in getting it done right. As you know, Unicode 3.0 which will be coming out early next year, really covers almost all the languages of everyone alive today; they have filled in the last gaps, they've got Burmese and the Maldive Islands, Sri Lanka, the places where the political difficulties were; they have several thousand extra Vietnamese and Chinese characters and so on. And Yi, and Mongolian, and native American — various Inuit and Algonquian languages — are all there now.

But each of these languages has special difficulties involved in the typesetting. It's not just a matter of getting the symbols; all kinds of ligatures and things must go in, and rewriting of characters. Many of the languages have no spaces between words, and special hyphenation conventions, and a total user community of a few thousand. Moreover, all the people who do use some of these languages are educated enough that writing in English gives them more job security; thus the more they do to make it possible for everybody else in their group to use the system, the less chance they have of being uniquely able to do anything. So it's going to be hard to support this commercially; it's surely going to be a volunteer effort. The effort is not only an order of magnitude more difficult than what I had to do, but it also has to be done pretty much as a labour of love, as I did it. So it looks to be a while before it could converge like that — not that it's impossible, but I myself wouldn't be in a position to bless it. All I can do is provide an example of one of the world's nearly bug-free programs so that other people can try to emulate the good points and correct the bad points.

Well, thank you very much. [*Applause*]

Philip Taylor: Don, I'd like to thank you very much indeed, on behalf, not only of the Committee of the U.K. TeX Users Group, but of every one of the members here who, I'm sure, are absolutely delighted that you have spoken to them. Thank you very much indeed for your time, for joining us. Jill, thank you very much indeed as well for coming along. It's been a great pleasure to have you both in our midst. We wish you a very safe and happy stay in the U.K. for the rest of your trip. Thank you very much indeed.

[Other interviews and Q&A sessions with Don are listed in the TUG Interview Corner, at `http://tug.org/interviews`. *Ed.*]

4

The TEX tuneup of 2008

[Published in *TUGboat* **29**:2, 2008]

I've written this note while going through the long, long file of bug reports and suggestions that were submitted during the years 2003–2007. You know that I am committed to keeping TEX and METAFONT as stable as possible, while also correcting serious blunders that are likely to be harmful if left as is. It is certainly not always obvious where to draw the line; I intend to keep drawing it as close to the existing implementations as I can, without feeling extremely guilty.

The index to *Digital Typography* lists eleven pages where the importance of stability is stressed, and I urge all maintainers of TEX and METAFONT to read them again every few years. Any object of nontrivial complexity is non-optimum, in the sense that it can be improved in some way (while still remaining non-optimum); therefore there's always a reason to change anything that isn't trivial. But one of TEX's principal advantages is the fact that it does not change — except for serious flaws whose correction is unlikely to affect more than a very tiny number of archival documents.

Let me give two examples. First, David Kastrup observes that TEX doesn't do the best possible rounding when it converts units. One inch is exactly 72.27 points, which is exactly 4736286.72 scaled points. When you say '`1in`', TEX converts it to 4736286sp; when you say '`72.27pt`', TEX converts it to 4736287sp, which is about 23.6 Ångstrom units closer to the truth. With a simple change to TEX §458, namely to add '`denom div 2`' before dividing by '`denom`', the rounding would be slightly better. But that would invalidate the line-break and page-break decisions of an enormous number of documents. It's unthinkable to change TEX in such a way today. But of course the authors of other systems should adopt superior methods when they want to.

Second, I recently installed METAPOST version 0.993, which corrected a bug in the calculation of the bounding box of its outputs. I'm a user of METAPOST, not a developer; but I'm sort of glad that the developers had fixed this bug. On the other hand it was a tremendous headache for me, because it affected nearly 200 of the illustrations for *The Art of Computer Programming*, and caused severe changes to the layouts of more than a dozen pages, even though the individual corrections to the box sizes were typically 2pt or less! I spent three days going over everything so that I could once again typeset the volumes of my main life's work. I couldn't reasonably insist that the METAPOST developers retain such a serious bug as a "feature". With TEX, on the other hand, it's a different story, because people's accumulated investment in TEX documents is more than a million times the total current investment in METAPOST documents. If a comparable bug had showed up in TEX, I would *not* have changed it.

Let me also observe that I never intended TEX to be immune to vicious "cracker attacks"; I only wish it to be robust under reasonable use by people who are trying to get productive work done. Almost every limit can be abused in extreme cases, and I don't think it useful to go to extreme pain to prevent such things. Computers have general protection mechanisms to keep buggy software from inflicting serious damage; TEX and METAFONT are far less buggy than the software for which such mechanisms were designed. For instances of the philosophy that I had while writing these programs, see for instance TEX §9 and MF §9, which say that I expected the programs to be run with arithmetic overflow interrupt turned on; also TEX §104: "TEX does not check for overflow when dimensions are added or subtracted ... the chance of overflow is so remote that such tests do not seem worthwhile"; MF §369 says that the total weight in a picture "will be less than 2^{31} unless the edge structure has more than 174,762 edges"; MF §558, "we shall assume that the coordinates are sufficiently non-extreme"; MF §930, "users aren't supposed to be monkeying around with really big values".

A proposal re file errors

I think the following change would be nice for the next versions of TEX, METAFONT, etc.: In place of the current message

`Please type another %s file name:`

produced by `prompt_file_name`, let's substitute

`Please type another %s file name (or quit):`

and then if the user's response is 'quit' we do the equivalent of control-C. If the response is null, let's give a help message.

This modification should be handled by change files, keeping the master files `tex.web` and `mf.web` and `whatever.web` as they are. I never have intended to control the aspects of user interaction on particular systems.

Maybe also introduce a finite loop, with '`(or quit)`' replaced by '`(or I'll quit)`' the third or fourth time. I agree that infinite loops are evil, and I'm sorry that `prompt_file_name` is invoked only within infinite loops in my own programs. If I had thought of this idea earlier, I'd have added a global variable like `max_prompt_repeats`, and initialized it to 3 or 4 just before those infinite loops; then `prompt_file_name` would decrement it, or give up if it's zero.

Another possibility is '`(or quit or retry)`', except the last time. That wording is a bit more suited to computer geeks, who have ideas about fixing things by repairing file permissions, etc.; if the user responds with either 'retry' or null, the intention is clearly to try again because of some reason to hope for success. Still, I prefer the non-geek version, because it reaches more people and enables the null-for-help option. Let the geeks type a few more keystrokes — they get satisfaction in other ways.

TEX

TEX version 3.1415926 corrects a few minor bugs, following major studies by David Fuchs. A summary of the noteworthy changes to the Pascal code in `tex.web` can be found near the end of the (long) file `errata/tex82.bug`. Here are the most significant ones, in decreasing order of importance:

1. Leaders with `\mskip` glue never worked properly; this feature has now been disallowed.

2. Error recovery was incorrect when an extra right brace appeared within a macro parameter.

3. TEX's inner loop now runs a bit faster.

4. The size of insert boxes is now displayed more accurately by `\showlists`.

5. A restriction on `TFM` files enforced by TFtoPL (namely that there must be at least one entry in each of the width, height, depth, and italic correction tables) is now enforced also by TEX, since noncompliance could cause a mess.

6. TEX used to leak four words of memory if arithmetic overflow occurred when `\multiply` or `\divide` was applied to `glue` or `muglue`.

7. The old `iniTeX` could leak four words of memory in another way (but at most four total), if "`last_glue`" pointed to a glue specification when the format file was created.

There's an undocumented feature, which is inconvenient to explain anywhere in *The TEXbook*: `\pagedepth` is cleared to zero when the current page disappears into `\box255`; but `\pagetotal`, `\pagestretch`, `\pagefilstretch`, `\pagefillstretch`,

`\pagefilllstretch`, and `\pageshrink` are zeroed later, when the current page becomes nonempty. (That's the time `\pagegoal` is set, and recorded in the log file with a `%%` line if you're tracing pages.) I don't recall why there is a discrepancy, but I certainly don't want to diddle with any of that logic at this late date.

Here are some other things that I don't want to touch:

i. David Kastrup found a glitch in plain TEX's footnote-splitting mechanism. Everything works according to the documentation in *The TEXbook* and I can't possibly make a change to such a sensitive part of TEX's logic at this late date. But his example is quite interesting, and I'd like to discuss it here for the benefit of people planning other systems.

Here's his construction (to be used with plain TEX):

```
\def\testpage#1{\dimen0=#1
  \vrule height .5\dimen0 depth .5\dimen0
  \quad #1\par
  Some text.\footnote*{A bigbreak follows...
                       \bigbreak
                       A bigbreak preceded.}
  \par\vfill\supereject}
\testpage{8.17in}
\testpage{8.23in}
\testpage{8.2in}
```

The first test page is an example where the entire footnote fits fine. In the second one, the footnote needs to be split; so two pages are generated, one with the first half of the footnote, as desired.

The third test page illustrates the problem: Plain TEX uses the worst of both strategies! Namely, it generates two pages, in which the first is underfull, while the second has the text and footnote that would have fit on the first page.

Why does plain TEX screw up here? Well, TEX knows that the footnote doesn't fit, when typeset at its natural height+depth of 36pt. So it tries to split it, by choosing a height threshold: It says to the `vsplit` routine, "Please give me your best break that doesn't exceed a height of 30.089pt." (That is what's left after we start with plain TEX's vsize of 8.9in and subtract the page-total-so-far, which is 8.2in for the `vrule`, plus 1pt of `lineskip`, plus 7.5pt for the height of 'Some text.', plus 12pt to separate the text from its first footnote.) The `vsplit` algorithm discovers two ways to break the footnote: One has height 8.5pt (the height of '* A bigbreak follows...'), depth 1.94444pt, and penalty −200 (at the `bigbreak`); the other has natural height 32.5pt, depth 3.5pt (which comes from a strut placed by plain TEX), and penalty −10000 (the force-out penalty at the very bottom of the footnote). This latter break is considered viable because 4pt of glue shrinkage is available to bring the height down to 30.089pt. Naturally `vsplit` chooses the latter alternative.

Then TEX does something dumb. It records the result of the split in the list of contributions to the current page, in such a way that the first part of the split will be included on the page only if there's room for its natural height+depth, namely 36pt in this case. (And in this case, the "first part of the split" actually turns out to be the whole footnote.) Therefore, when TEX next finds a legal breakpoint, the current page limit has been exceeded, and the line with its footnote is deemed not to be permissible. The previous break, which leaves an underfull vbox, is chosen instead of "overfilling" the page — even though there is really enough shrinkability to bring the page back to size.

As I said, it's too late now to correct my age-old faulty reasoning. If I'd known about the problem twenty years ago, I may well have decided to make the change that seems most appropriate to me today, which is this:

```
@x module 974
    best_height_plus_depth:=cur_height+prev_dp;
@y
    best_height_plus_depth:=cur_height+prev_dp;
    if (best_height_plus_depth>h+prev_dp)
      and (b<awful_bad) then
      best_height_plus_depth:=h+prev_dp;
@z
```

In other words, the log file (with `tracingpages=1`) now gets the line

```
% split254 to 30.08878,36.0 p=-10000
```

but after that patch it would instead say

```
% split254 to 30.08878,33.58878 p=-10000
```

and the footnote would wind up on the first page where it belongs.

When I made the mistake ages ago, I probably wasn't thinking of shrinkability inside the footnote, only in the "virtual" amount of space within `\skip254` that separates the text from its footnotes. Indeed, the present problem goes away if one sets `\skip254=12pt minus 8pt`. But that workaround would be appropriate only for this particular example.

ii. Section 798 could be made more robust with "`until q=cur_align`" moved down one line. Implementors can put this into a change file if they like.

iii. The format `plain.tex` leaves `\box0=\hbox{\tenex B}`; and it also defines `\\` to be a macro such that "`\\10pt`" expands to "`10`" (for example). I could have cleaned these up by saying something like

```
{\setbox1=\box0} \let\\=\undefined
```

but I decided not to change it, since `plain.tex` is so widely used as is.

iv. Frank Mittelbach reported a construction of Morten Høgholm Pedersen:

```
\parindent=0pt
\setbox0=\hbox{p} \hsize=\wd0
\discretionary{m-}{h}{p}\par
```

It gives an overfull box, because TEX doesn't see any feasible breakpoint. (More precisely, the pre-break part exceeds the line width, and TEX doesn't look ahead to see if some fairy godmother is going to save us.) Thus TEX is resigned to making an overfull box, and it takes the only legal breakpoint it knows.

This must be considered a feature of TEX's line-break algorithm. Namely, a discretionary break is normally never taken when the pre-break part would make an overfull box; but it is always taken in the unusual case that no other feasible break is possible (without looking ahead at the third, "unbroken" alternative of the discretionary). A problem can arise only if an unhyphenated word is actually shorter than its first hyphenated fragment. What, me worry?

Amusingly, if you put the line

```
\spaceskip=0pt plus 1fill
  \discretionary{p}{\kern-2em}{}
```

before the other discretionary, you get two p's and nothing overfull.

v. Jonathan Kew mentioned some of the surprising effects that occur when you try to do things in the command line (or in the very first line of TEX's input, at the `**` prompt). There are many, many such.

Before TEX knows the job name, it outputs just to the terminal. Log file output won't happen until an `\input` command has occurred, or input line one has been processed, whichever comes first, because the log file is given its name at that time.

For example,

```
**\showhyphens{whatever}
```

will show '`what-ever`' on the terminal, but not in the log file. Same for

```
**\showhyphens{whatever} \input foo
```

but in this case the log file is called `foo.log` instead of `texput.log`. With

```
**\input foo \showhyphens{whatever}
```

you see '`what-ever`' also in `foo.log`.

plain TEX format

Version 3.141592653 of `plain.tex` is identical to version 3.14159265, except that `\errorstopmode` is no longer invoked by the `\tracingall` and `\loggingall` macros. (That mistake had been in `plain.tex` for more than 25 years, and I thank David Kastrup for the wakeup call.)

METAFONT

Turning now to METAFONT, Thorsten Dahlheimer gave the whole program a much-needed scrutiny and came up with a number of bugs that have now been corrected in version 2.718281. (Incidentally, he has also given me invaluable help finding mistakes in the darker corners of *TAOCP*.) Only one of those bugs was serious enough to affect real programs with high probability; the others are the sorts of things that a good nitpicker will spot when reading code, although the actual misbehavior requires weird scenarios. As usual, you can find details of the significant changes to Pascal code in the file `errata/mf84.bug`. The complete source file `mf.web` shows many instances of improved commentary.

1. The serious bug arose from user input such as

```
boolean b[]; b1=true=b2;
```

earlier versions of METAFONT would go into an infinite loop from such constructions, so evidently nobody ever writes code like this. (Strings, paths, and pictures have similar problems, not just booleans.) No problem would occur if the statement had been "`b1=b2=true`" instead. I forgot to include one instruction in my program, and it's a glaring error in section 1003.

This bug is also in the METAPOST source, `mp.web`, which I assume somebody else will fix. Whoever does that should also look carefully at the other changes just made to `mf.web`, since so much of the code is common to both.

2. There also were problems in the `TFM` files when extremely large characters or dimensions were present. For example, from

```
mode:=lowres; mode_setup; designsize:=10pt#;
beginchar("!",160pt#,-160pt#,160pt#);
  endchar; end
```

you get a `TFM` file with a bad character width and depth, because of an off-by-one error in my code. (TFtoPL doesn't complain about the character height, which violates some but not all of the documentation of TFM files: A `fix_word` is supposed to lie between -2048 and $2048-2^{-20}$, inclusive, but *The METAFONTbook* says that no TFM dimension should result in the `fix_word` value -2048. TEX has no problem inputting that value.)

3. Another TFM problem was tweaked with ultralarge design sizes:

```
fontmaking:=1; designsize:=2000;
  fontdimen 2: 3000;
  shipout nullpicture; end
```

used to set `fontdimen 2` (the SPACE parameter) to be about 32000 points. The correct behavior is to reduce `fontdimen 2` to just less than 2048 points.

4. Weird behavior could previously occur with

```
transform T;
T=identity xscaled 4 yscaled 3 rotated 180;
pickup pencircle transformed T;
show currentpen;
```

which always came out correctly without the (redundant) rotation by 180.

5. Another bug arose in code fragments like

```
string a.b; a.b="lost"; outer a;
  numeric a.c; showvariable a;
```

the `string a.b` was indeed now lost. (METAPOST probably fails in the same way.)

6. METAFONT now checks that serial numbers don't overflow. Actually I had recommended that the program always be run with arithmetic integer overflow trapped; but this doesn't seem to be current practice. If a user creates 2^{25} distinct numeric variables, the "`METAFONT capacity exceeded`" error now occurs; formerly, this would have caused arithmetic overflow. (Well, this correction was actually made already in TEX-live change files some years ago; I've now introduced it into the master file `mf.web`, in a slightly different way.)

Not a bug: The `init_gf` procedure has an assignment to `str_start[str_ptr+1]` that looks like it could cause a segmentation fault if `str_ptr=max_strings`. Actually, however, that can't happen. (The test "`str_ptr+3>max_strings`" in `end_name`, together with the fact that `area_delimiter=0` in that procedure because `cur_area=""`, provides the extra breathing space.) But I changed `init_gf` anyway.

Anomalies that won't be changed: Autorounding does not work properly when filling certain nonconvex shapes, such as

```
pickup makepen((-.6,0)--(.6,0)--cycle);
filldraw (2,0){up}..(0,1){down}..%
  (1,0){down}..(0,-1){down}..cycle
```

at point `(1,0)`. Pens whose width and height are not integers are deprecated; there's no point cluttering up the code with stuff that benefits only them.

One of METAFONT's (and METAPOST's) most interesting algorithms is the way it chooses control points and directions for paths that are partially specified. I ran into a curious glitch some years ago when preparing an illustration for my book *Selected Papers on Computer Languages*: The two paths

```
    (0,0){dir45}...(15,0)...(0,0){dir150}
and (0,0){dir-45}...(15,0)...(0,0){dir-150}
```

turn out to have amazingly different shapes. (The first one twists around almost unbelievably, while the second looks reasonable.) I tracked this down to the equations in METAFONT's "`solve_choices`" routine, which chooses the desired "turning angle" at the point `(15,0)`. In both cases this value, `psi[1]`, is set to `n_arg(-983040,0)`; here −983040 is the internal (scaled) representation of −15, and `n_arg` is supposed to determine the value of `angle(-15,0)`. [See page 67 of *The METAFONTbook*.] The answer is 180, which is appropriate in the second case, but the first case really wants the answer to be −180.

Computer Modern

I made a noticeable change to the shape of one (and only one) letter in the CM family, namely the calligraphic F. The new one has a slightly different swash, which pleases me more when I look at it in *The Art of Computer Programming*. The change is small, yet it would be nice if people would remake the Type 1 versions of the fonts that use `calu.mf`, namely `cmsy*` and `cmbsy*`.

The lowercase Greek nu could develop a tiny notch at the bottom, especially at high resolutions of boldface versions (brought to my attention by Charles Duan, who conjectured its existence by reading the source code!). So I corrected that problem.

Duan also found a few other places where the source code was logically wrong in `greekl.mf`. I fixed those too. However, those changes don't actually show up in the generated font, since the differences in point positions are minuscule.

Karel Piška noticed that the bulbs of lowercase a and c are positioned rather differently when the "`blacker`" parameter of a mode varies. (He blamed it on varying resolution, but that's because my code was obscure.) In those characters I essentially try to move strokes apart so that there's twice as much white space as the thickness of the pen; therefore a `blacker` pen makes the strokes go further apart. My logic was faulty, because the "`blacker`" setting was intended to compensate for differences in the device that make its apparent pen width too small, thereby making the actual appearance after printing only as black as it would have been on an ideal device; increasing "`blacker`" by 1 shouldn't make me reposition any strokes. Yet I do actually reposition them, on the lowercase a, by roughly 2 pixels per unit of `blacker`! And the bulb on c is positioned to be like that of a. Still, the repositioned bulbs look OK, and I'm happy to continue forever with this wart in the design.

TEXware

TFtoPL version 3.2 is identical to version 3.1 except that a (missing) newline character now appears after one of the warning messages.

Computers & Typesetting

Dozens of corrections were made to Volumes A, B, C, D, and E of the books *Computers & Typesetting*, bringing everything up to date with respect to the latest sources. (This includes *The TEXbook*, which is a paperback Volume A, and *The METAFONTbook*, which is a paperback Volume C.) Copies of the corrected books won't be available for sale until the publisher's stock of already-printed volumes is depleted; but I've prepared detailed errata from which you can make hardcopy inserts to paste into the books you have.

Summary

All of the results of my changes appear in the following files:

`tex/texbook.tex` % source file for *The TEXbook*
`tex/tex.web` % complete master file for TEX in Pascal
`tex/trip.fot` % torture test terminal output
`tex/tripin.log` % torture test first log file

```
tex/trip.log % torture test second log file
tex/trip.typ % torture test output of DVItype
texware/tftopl.web % complete master file for TFtoPL in Pascal
mf/mfbook.tex % source file for The METAFONTbook
mf/mf.web % complete master file for METAFONT in Pascal
mf/trap* % (namely trap.fot, trapin.log, trap.log, trap.typ, trap.pl)
mf/trap.fot % torture test terminal output
mf/trapin.log % torture test first log file
mf/trap.log % torture test second log file
mf/trap.typ % torture test output of GFtype
mf/trap.pl % torture test output of TFtoPL
cm/calu.mf % master source file for calligraphic capital letters
cm/greekl.mf % master source file for lowercase greek letters
cm/symbol.mf % master source file for special symbols
errata/errata.ten % changes to Volumes ABCDE before 2001
errata/errata.eleven % changes to Volumes ABCDE in 2001
errata/errata.tex % changes to Volumes ABCDE since the 2001 boxed set
errata/tex82.bug % changes to tex.web since the beginning
errata/mf84.bug % changes to mf.web since the beginning
errata/cm85.bug % changes to Computer Modern metafont sources since 1985
```

These files are available in directory `pub/tex/dist` of the ftp server `cs.stanford.edu`, which accepts "`anonymous`" as a login name. They are a subset of the files in `pub/tex/dist/tex08.tar.gz`, which you can compare to `pub/tex/dist/tex03.tar.gz` if you like. Hopefully they will be easy to incorporate into the major distributions of TEX, and they will presumably soon be available on CTAN.

In general the changes can be characterized as a general cleanup, especially to the documentation. The new versions don't affect old documents, except when the existing behavior was seriously incorrect. (And except for the fact that TEX will often run a bit faster now.)

To do this revision I waded through more than 600 K bytes of text files, not counting the binary `.pdf` and `.png` files that were also submitted. Barbara Beeton faithfully compiled all of this material during the years 2003–2007, and organized it so that my task wasn't hopeless. She had many volunteers helping to separate wheat from chaff; needless to say, I'm extremely grateful for all of this assistance.

The total number of independent topics about which I had to make a decision, after they had come through the filtering process, was approximately 335. Some of these needed several days of thought and careful study; some of them needed only a few seconds. More than a hundred of them were nontrivial, and I did my best.

So now I send best wishes to the whole TEX community, as I leave for vacation to the land of *TAOCP* — until 31 December 2013. Au revoir!

I intend to be fully responsible
for all changes to these systems
for the rest of my life.
I will periodically study reports of apparent bugs,
and I will decide whether changes need to be made.

— DONALD KNUTH, *TUGboat* (1990)

KUG 2005
Wuhan China

Part II
Early participants

In this part of the book we reproduce one paper by each of (alphabetically) David Fuchs, John Hobby, Frank Liang, Michael Plass, Oren Patashnik, Tomas Rokicki, Luis Trabb Pardo, and Howard Trickey, most of whom we expect to be present with Donald Knuth at the 2010 TUG annual conference in San Francisco. Each has a chapter with a brief biographical note, the bibliography of their papers from *TUGboat*, and the reprinted paper.

Ignacio Zabala is the first author of the Trabb Pardo paper (page 85). We were unable to contact him and, thus, regretfully could not invite him to the 2010 conference. Zabala has no other papers in *TUGboat*; his Ph.D. dissertation was *Interacting with Graphic Objects*, and his advisor was Donald Knuth. Zabala made a major contribution in those early days of TEX as described in the paper with Trabb Pardo and in the following quotes by Knuth.

There were also various calligraphers and font designers involved at Stanford during those early days of TEX.

Hermann Zapf's influence on Knuth and his involvement with Knuth has been well documented in several papers, for example, those reproduced in Knuth's 1999 *Digital Typography* book.

Knuth has often acknowledged the help and influence of font designer Matthew Carter, though he was not at Stanford.

Charles Bigelow, Kris Holmes, and Richard Southall also worked close by and influenced Knuth or were involved with his font- and METAFONT development efforts. Bigelow started a Master's program in digital typography at Stanford. He was at Stanford for thirteen years and taught type design, typography, and the history and theory of writing. In a 1984 *TUGboat* article, "A course on METAFONT programming," Knuth describes a course that he jointly taught with Bigelow and Southall which was attended by what he calls "four dozen brave students." Southall and Bigelow were on the Stanford faculty.

5

David Fuchs

David Fuchs arrived at Stanford in 1978 to study for a Ph.D. in computer science. When he saw a notice that Donald Knuth was looking for help on the TeX project, he jumped at the chance to work with Knuth and to work on software that might get widespread use.[1]

Initially David worked on porting the TeX78 code written in the SAIL language from Knuth's Waits operating system to the TOPS-20 operating system. There were several source files, and the `TEXOUT` module handled output to an XGP printer. In 1980, they got a new Versatec printer, and David conceived and designed the first version of the DVI (device independent) output for TeX and, it appears, also wrote the DVI-to-Versatec driver.

As Knuth and his students rewrote TeX (and METAFONT) in the new `WEB` language, David helped with various porting issues, and he wrote the DVI-to-CRS software for the Alphatype CRS phototypesetter.

As shown in the bibliography below, David wrote reports on TeX project progress throughout this period, stopping only in 1986 when Knuth wanted to wind down his involvement in the TeX project. David was a member of the TUG board of directors from 1981–1990.

After Stanford, David was involved in several high tech start-ups. He remains proud of his involvement with TeX, the contributions it made to the state-of-the-art, and its longevity.

TUGboat bibliography

The format of TeX's DVI files [**1**:1, October 1980]

Erratum: The format of TeX's DVI files [**2**:1, February 1981]

TeX font metric files [**2**:1, February 1981]

The format of TeX's DVI files, version 1 [**2**:2, July 1981]

Output device news flash (APS-5 and Linotron 202) [**2**:2, July 1981]

The format of PXL files [**2**:3, November 1981]

News from the home front (Stanford) [**2**:3, November 1981]

The format of TeX's DVI files [**3**:2, October 1982]

News from Stanford [**3**:2, October 1982]

TeXhax summary [**4**:1, April 1983]

News from all over [**4**:1, April 1983]

TeX vs. INITeX [**4**:2, September 1983]

TeXhax summary [**4**:2, September 1983]

News from the TeX project [**4**:2, September 1983]

Observations on TeX from a divergent viewpoint: Comments, response, and reresponse [**4**:2, September 1983]

News from the TeX project [**5**:1, May 1984]

News from the TeX project [**5**:2, November 1984]

News from the TeX project [**7**:1, March 1986]

[1]This biographical note is taken from David Fuchs' TUG interview (`http://tug.org/interviews/fuchs.html`) and other sources.

The format of TeX's DVI files: Version 1

[Published in *TUGboat* **2**:2, July 1981]

When TeX compiles a document, it produces an output file that contains specifications of how TeX has decided the formatted text should appear in hard copy. These output files are known as '`.DVI`' files, which stands for 'device independent'. For instance, running TeX and telling it to `\input dviinf` will cause TeX to look for a file called `DVIINF.TEX`, read it, and produce an output file called `DVIINF.DVI`, which is a `.DVI` file. This document describes the format of `.DVI` files in detail, giving all the specifications along with examples.

A `.DVI` file contains information about where characters go on pages. The format is such that there are those who say that almost any reasonable device can be driven by a program that takes `.DVI` files as input. In particular, a `.DVI` file can be printed on the Xerox Dover, Xerox Graphics Printer (XGP), Varian, Versatec, Canon and Alphatype at the Stanford CS Dept., depending on what spooler it is passed to.

The `.DVI` file is a stream of 8-bit bytes, packed in computer words high-order byte first. If the computer word length is not evenly divisible by 8, then the extra bits at the low-order end of each word will be unused. The first byte in a `.DVI` file is byte number zero, the next is number one, etc. For example, on Stanford's 36-bit word machines, byte number 0 is in the highest order eight bits of the first word in a `.DVI` file, while byte number 7 is in the twelfth through fifth least significant bits of the second word in the file; and the least significant four bits in every word are zero.

A `.DVI` file is actually a series of **commands**. A **command** consists of one byte containing the **command**'s unique number, followed by a number (possibly zero) of **parameters** to the **command**. A given **command** always has the same number of **parameters**. These **parameters** may take from one to four bytes each, but a given **parameter** of a given **command** always takes the same number of bytes. Some **parameters** may sometimes be negative, in which case two's complement representation is used. The complete list of **commands**, with a description of all the `.DVI` **commands** and their **parameters**, is below. The reader is encouraged to refer to the **command** list while reading the various examples in this document.

In the **command** descriptions, a lower case letter with a [bracketed] number following it means that the **command** has a **parameter** that is that number of bytes long. An X2 **command**, for instance, is 3 bytes long, the first byte of which has the decimal value 144, the second and third of which give the distance to move to the right. If the second byte $= S$ and the third $= T$, then the distance to move is 2^8S+T (but if the high order bit of S is a one, then the distance to move is 2^8S+T-2^{16}, considering S and T as being in the range $[0..255]$).

The `.DVI` file contains a number of **pages** followed by a **postamble**. A **page** consists of a BOP **command**, followed by lots of other **commands** that tell where the characters on the page go, followed by an EOP **command**. Each EOP **command** is immediately followed by another BOP **command**, or by the PST **command**, which means that there are no more **pages** in the file, and the remaining bytes in the `.DVI` file are the **postamble**. Remember that TeX really doesn't have an official knowledge of **page** numbers (although it does print the value of `\count0` on your terminal as it outputs each **page** on the assumption that some meaningful number is there), so the only thing that can be said about the ordering of pages in a `.DVI` file is: The order in which **page**s come in a `.DVI` file is the same order in which TEX constructed them, which is the same order in which the TEX user specified them. Any blank or nonexistent **page** from a TEX job might not be in the `.DVI` file at all. If we consider the **page** number to be the value of `count0`, then the **page** following **page** number 34 in a `.DVI` file might well be **page** number −5.

Some **parameter**s of `.DVI` **command**s are **pointer**s. A **pointer** is simply a byte number as discussed above. A **pointer** itself is 4 bytes long. For example, a BOP **command**'s last **parameter** (`p[4]`) is the BOP's **previous page pointer**. This parameter is the number of the byte in which the previous **page**'s BOP command begins. In particular, the *second* **page**'s BOP **command**'s **previous page pointer parameter** (`p[4]`) is always zero, since the first **page**'s BOP is always in byte zero in a `.DVI` file. If the first **page** in a `.DVI` file had only a BOP and EOP **command**, then the *third* **page**'s BOP's **previous page pointer** would be 46, since the first **page**'s BOP **command** takes bytes zero through 44, the first **page**'s EOP is byte 45, so the *second* **page**'s BOP is in byte 46.

When a `.DVI`-reading program reads the **command**s for a **page**, it should keep track of the **current font**. This can be done with a single integer variable, the value of which will always lie in the range $[0..2^{32}-2]$. The value of the **current font** is changed only by FONT and FONTNUM **commands**. Whenever a **command** occurs in the `.DVI` file that causes a character to be set on the **page**, the character is implicitly from the **current font**.

Likewise, the program should keep track of the **current position on the page**. The **current position on the page** is like a cursor on the **page**; whenever a character or rule is set, it gets put at the **current position on the page**. The **current position on the page** is just two numbers—which are called **horizontal coordinate** and **vertical coordinate**. Moving to the right on a **page** is represented by an increase in **horizontal coordinate**, while moving down is an increase in **vertical coordinate**. The upper-left-hand corner of the **page** is **horizontal coordinate** = **vertical coordinate** = 0 (i.e., our system is slightly non-cartesian). Both **coordinates** are given in rsu's (ridiculously small units), where $1\text{rsu} = 10^{-7}\text{meter}$. This is so that accumulated errors will be insignificant even in the worst imaginable case (a "box" many feet long). The **current position on the page** is moved about by the commands W0, W2, W3, W4, X0, X2, X3, X4, Y0, Y2, Y3, Y4, Z0, Z2, Z3 and Z4: The **vertical coordinate** is changed by Y and Z **commands**, while the **horizontal coordinate** is changed by W and X **commands**. (The value of **horizontal coordinate** can also change as a side effect of setting a character or rule (VERTCHAR and VERTRULE **commands**)—the **current position on the page** moves right the natural width of the character or rule set. The POP **command** may also change **current position on the page**.)

So, whoever or whatever reads a `.DVI` file might have three variables, F, H and V, to keep track of the **current font** and the **current position on the page**. Four more variables are also called for: **w-amount**, **x-amount**, **y-amount**, and **z-amount**. These variables hold not locations, but distances (in rsu's). The **amount** variables are used in `.DVI` files to move the **current position on the page** around: The **commands** X0 and W0 add **x-amount** and **w-amount** to **horizontal coordinate**, respectively, while Y0 and Z0 add **y-amount** or **z-amount** to **vertical coordinate**, respectively. There are also a number of **command**s that change the value of **w-amount**, **x-amount**, **y-amount** or **z-amount** (W2, W3, W4, X2, X3, X4, Y2, Y3, Y4, Z2, Z3 and Z4; these commands also change **horizontal coordinate** or **vertical**

coordinate). Actually, the `.DVI`-reading program must have a stack that can hold **horizontal coordinates** and **vertical coordinates**, as well as **w-**, **x-**, **y-**, and **z-amounts**. These six values always get pushed and popped together, and a reasonable maximum stack depth might be about 200 (times six, since six items get pushed at once). As each **page** starts, a `.DVI` reading program should set the **amount** variables to zero. The stack should be empty. The initial value of F doesn't matter, since *every* **page** of a `.DVI` file must have a FONT or FONTNUM **command** before any **command** that will set a character (the HORZCHAR and VERTCHAR **commands**). Note that F is *not* pushed and popped.

A program called `DVITYP` is available that takes any `.DVI` file and prints a readable description of its contents, together with error messages if the file is not in the correct format.

. . . .

Command Name
  Command Bytes
  Description

VERTCHAR0
  0
  Set character number 0 from the **current font** such that its reference point is at the **current position on the page**, and then increment **horizontal coordinate** by the character's width.

VERTCHAR1
  1
  Set character number 1, etc.

⋮ ⋮

VERTCHAR127
  127
  Set character number 127, etc.

NOP 128
  No-op, do nothing, ignore. Note that NOPs come *between* **commands**, they may not come between a **command** and its **parameters**, or between two **parameters**.

BOP 129 `c0`[4] `c1`[4] ... `c9`[4] `p`[4]
  Beginning of **page**. The **parameter** `p` is a **pointer** to the BOP **command** of the *previous* **page** in the `.DVI` file (where the *first* BOP in a `.DVI` file has a `p` of −1, by convention). The ten `c`'s hold the values of TeX's ten `\counter`s at the time this **page** was output.

EOP 130
  The end of all **commands** for the **page** has been reached. The number of PUSH **commands** on this **page** should equal the number of POPs.

PUSH 132

Push the current values of **horizontal coordinate** and **vertical coordinate**, and the current **w-**, **x-**, **y-**, and **z-amount**s onto the stack, but don't alter them (so an X0 after a PUSH will get to the same spot that it would have had it had been given just before the PUSH).

POP 133

Pop the **z-**, **y-**, **x-**, and **w-amount**s, and **vertical coordinate** and **horizontal coordinate** off the stack. At no point in a `.DVI` file will there have been more POPs than PUSHes.

HORZRULE

135 `h`[4] `w`[4]

Typeset a rule of height `h` and width `w`, with its bottom left corner at the **current position on the page**. If either `h` ≤ 0 or `w` ≤ 0, no rule should be set.

VERTRULE

134 `h`[4] `w`[4]

Same as HORZRULE, but also increment **horizontal coordinate** by `w` when done (even if `h` ≤ 0 or `w` ≤ 0).

HORZCHAR

136 `c`[1]

Set character `c` just as if we'd gotten the VERTCHAR`c` **command**, but don't change the **current position on the page**. Note that `c` must be in the range [0..127].

FONT 137 `f`[4]

Set **current font** to `f`. Note that this **command** is not currently used by TEX — it is only needed if `f` is greater than 63, because of the FONTNUM **commands** below. Large font numbers are intended for use with oriental alphabets and for (possibly large) illustrations that are to appear in a document; the maximum legal number is $2^{32} - 2$.

X2 144 `m`[2]

Move right `m` rsu's by adding `m` to **horizontal coordinate**, and put `m` into **x-amount**. Note that `m` is in 2's complement, so this could actually be a move to the left.

X3 143 `m`[3]

Same as X2 (but has a 3 byte long `m` **parameter**).

X4 142 `m`[4]

Same as X2 (but has a 4 byte long `m` **parameter**).

X0 145

Move right **x-amount** (which can be negative, etc).

W2 140 `m`[2]
The same as the X2 **command** (i.e., alters **horizontal coordinate**), but alter **w-amount** rather than **x-amount**, so that doing a W0 **command** can have different results than doing an X0 **command**.

W3 139 `m`[3]
As above.

W4 138 `m`[4]
As above.

W0 141
Move right **w-amount**.

Y2 148 `n`[2]
Same idea, but now it's "down" rather than "right", so **vertical coordinate** changes, as does **y-amount**.

Y3 147 `n`[3]
As above.

Y4 146 `n`[4]
As above.

Y0 149
Guess.

Z2 152 `m`[2]
Another downer. Affects **vertical coordinate** and **z-amount**.

Z3 151 `m`[3]

Z4 150 `m`[4]

Z0 153
Guess again.

FONTNUM0
154
Set **current font** to 0.

FONTNUM1
155
Set **current font** to 1.

⋮ ⋮

FONTNUM63
217
Set **current font** to 63.

PST   131 p[4] n[4] d[4] m[4] h[4] w[4]
Fontdef Fontdef ... Fontdef
-1[4] q[4] i[1] 223[?]
The **postamble** starts here. See below for the full explanation of the **parameters** of the **postamble**.

Commands 218–255 are currently undefined and will not be output by TEX.

The PST **command**, which is always the last command in a .DVI file, is somewhat special. The **parameter** p is a **pointer** to the BOP of the final **page** in the .DVI file. The **parameters** n and d are the numerator and denominator of a fraction by which all the dimensions in the .DVI file should be multiplied by to get rsu's (TEX always outputs a 1 for each of these values, they are included in .DVI format to allow other text systems to conveniently output .DVI files). The **parameter** m is the overall magnification requested by par12 in the TEX job (par12 is unitless, and is 1000 times the desired magnification). Next come h and w, which are the height of the tallest **page**, and the width of the widest (both in rsu's).

Next in the postamble come the **font definitions**, one for each font used in the job (i.e., each FONT and FONTNUM **command** in a .DVI file must refer to a **font number** that has a **font definition**). The format of a **font definition** can be considered to be:

fnum[4] fchk[4] fmag[4] fnamlen[1] fnam[fnamlen]

The **font number** is held in fnum. The **font checksum** (from the font's TFM file) is in fchk. The **parameter** fmag holds the **font magnification** (1000 times the 'at size' of the font divided by its 'design size' (or just 1000 if there was no 'at' specification for the font)). Next comes the byte fnamlen, which is the number of characters in the **font name**, followed by the **font name**, one ASCII character per byte (right justified). Note that the font name includes a directory only if the font is not in the standard default library directory. From the definitions of the **parameters** of the PST command, note that the end of the **font definitions** is marked by a **font number** of -1 (which is *not* a legal font number). The four bytes following this phony **font number** constitute the **parameter** q, which is a **pointer** to the PST **command** (i.e., the beginning of the postamble). Next is a single byte **parameter** i (called the ID byte). Currently, the ID byte should always have a value of 1; it will be changed to 2 on the next incompatible release of .DVI format in 1990. Finally, there is some number (at least 4) of bytes whose value is 223 (base ten = '337 octal).

The idea of the q **pointer** at the end of the **postamble** is that a .DVI reading program can start at the end of the .DVI file, skipping backwards over the 223's, until it finds the ID byte. Then it can back up 4 bytes, read q, and then do a random seek to that byte number within the .DVI file. Now the **postamble** can be read from start to finish, while storing away the names and magnifications of all the fonts. Now the program can jump to the start of the .DVI file and read it sequentially. The reason for reading the **postamble** first is that to figure where the characters on a page go, the .DVI reading program must know the widths of the characters (see the VERTCHAR commands' description above). To find the widths, the .DVI reader must know the names of the fonts so it can get their widths from a TFM or VNT (or some other kind of font) file. But TEX can't put out all the font names until the end of the .DVI file because new fonts can appear anywhere in the TEX job. If **font definitions** were scattered throughout the .DVI file, then a spooler that read .DVI files would have to read all the pages of the `.DVI` file, even if the user only wanted the last page printed. The decision to put the **font definitions** in the **postamble** was based on these considerations, and the fact that just about any reasonable systems language allows random access. Unfortunately, standard PASCAL does not offer this feature. If it is absolutely necessary for a `.DVI` reading program to be written in standard PASCAL, then it either must make two passes over the `.DVI` file, or TEX must be doctored to output *two* files: the regular `.DVI` file, plus a PST file, which contains only the **postamble**. So far, there have been no reports of any installation of TEX that required this kind of kludge.

A few words on magnification: If you have a TEX document that does not mention any 'true' dimensions, then if you change just its `magnify` statement, the `.DVI` file produced by TEX will change in just *one* place — the word in the postamble that records the requested magnification. The idea is that any spooler that reads the `.DVI` file will multiply *all* dimensions in the `.DVI` file by the magnification, thus the default magnification in the `.DVI` file may be easily overridden at spooling time. So, if the document specifies `\magnify{1200}`, a `\vskip 34cm` will be recorded in the `.DVI` file as $.34 \times 10^7$ rsu's of white space, but the spooler will multiply this by 1.2, making 40.8 centimeters of white space on output. If the user tells the spooler to use a magnification of 1000 rather than the 1200 in the `.DVI` file, then the output will have 34cm of white space. If a dimension in the document is specified as being 'true', then TEX divides the distance specified by the prevailing magnification, so that when a spooler looks at the `.DVI` file and multiplies by the magnification, it gets back the original distance. So, if we `\vskip 24truecm` while the magnification is 1200, TEX puts out `.DVI` **commands** that specifies 20 centimeters of white space. An output spooler that reads this `.DVI` file then puts $20 \times 1.2 = 24$cm of white space on its output. Of course, 'true' dimensions will come out 'false' if the spooler is told to override the magnification.

Font magnification goes one step further. Assume for a moment that the overall magnification is 1000. Now, if a TEX job specifies `\font A=CMR10 at 15pt`, say, that font's magnification is recorded as 1500 in its **font definition**. When a spooler reads this `.DVI` file, it will try to use the file `CMR10.150VNT` (or `CMR10.150ANT`, depending on the device), which is just like `CMR10.100VNT`, but the dimensions of all its characters were multiplied by 1.5 before they were digitized. An uppercase 'W' in CMR10 is 10pt wide, but CMR10 at 15pt has a 15pt wide 'W', so after VERTCHAR87 is seen, **horizontal coordinate** is increased by (15pt) $\times$ (254000rsu/72.27pt). Overall magnification is taken into account after all other calculations; for example, at magnification 1200 the font `CMR10.120VNT` would be used. Note that if the user had asked for `cmr10 at 15truept`, the factors would cancel out so that `CMR10.150VNT` would be the font chosen regardless of magnification. The magnification factor is given times 100 in the font file name so that roundoff error due to several multiplications will not affect the search for a font with characters of the right size. This convention about font file names is merely a suggestion, of course, it is not part of the `.DVI` format per se.

Appendix: Comparison between version 0 and version 1.

Note that `.DVI` files have an ID byte at the end of the **postamble**, which tells what version they are. The changes since version 0 are:

DVI files now use the *upper* bits in a word on machines whose word size isn't evenly divisible by 8. The BOP command has *ten* `\counter` parameters. The size of rsu's has changed to be 10^{-7}meter. The postamble has changed to include overall magnification as well as a fraction that allows use of non-rsu dimensions. Font checksum and magnification are new, as is the convention about default directory name. Font descriptions in the postamble give the length of font names rather than delimiting them with a quoting character. The old zero ID byte is now a one.

Some ideas for version 2.

Although 1990 is still a ways off, we are currently expecting that version 2 of `.DVI` files will differ in the following ways:

The ID byte will be 2. The `q` bytes of the postamble will be preceded by '`s`[2]' where `s` is the maximum stack depth (excess of pushes over pops) needed to process this file.

. . . a file with a format particular to TEX
that is known as DVI (acronym of device independent).
This file format, compared with formats such as PDF, PostScript, and DOC,
is an extremely simple and abstract page description.
. . . After the blizzard of LATEX and TEX commands that we have just seen,
now we shall observe the total calm that reigns in a DVI file.

— YANNIS HARALAMBOUS, *Fonts & Encodings* (2007)

Another stroke of luck
was to have outstanding research associates
like David Fuchs and John Hobby.

— DONALD KNUTH, *TUGboat* (1986)

6

John Hobby

John Hobby grew up in the Seattle area and received his Bachelor's degree in mathematics and computer science from the University of Washington.[1]

He started Ph.D. word at Stanford in 1980 where he and lots of other people in the computer science department used TEX78. In time he became involved in testing new versions of TEX as Donald Knuth developed the system we know today.

John also became involved with METAFONT's predecessor, MF79, and worked with Gu Guoan (whom Knuth brought from China as a visitor to Stanford) to develop a prototype set of Chinese characters, as described in his first *TUGboat* article (see bibliography below).

Knuth was John's thesis advisor, METAFONT's polynomial pens were an important part of his 1985 thesis entitled *Digitized Brush Trajectories*. John contributed various other algorithms to the development of METAFONT, including METAFONT's system of cubic spline curves. John recalls that he and Knuth worked together pretty closely while Knuth was developing METAFONT, in an unusual teacher-student collaboration in that John mostly designed algorithms and Knuth wrote all the production code.

After Stanford, in 1985, John joined Bell Labs in New Jersey. While there it occurred to him that Metafont could be retargeted to output PostScript, making it easier for him to draw figures for his research papers. His research figures were more mathematical and less artistic than a font, and a Metafont-like approach would be easier than calculating a lot of coordinates and typing them in computer files.

John worked on METAPOST on and off for about two years, starting in 1990 (despite the fact that his first METAFONT paper was dated 1989), and then distributed it widely within AT&T. For the next couple of years METAPOST was distributed outside of AT&T only under non-disclosure agreements, but finally in 1995 a public domain distribution was made.

As John could not justify continuing to do work on METAFONT on Bell Labs time beyond a few bug fixes and minor improvements, he was glad when Taco Hoekwater and other members of the current METAPOST development group took over maintenance and significant new developments.

John continues to work at the same place in New Jersey, although now it is part of Alcatel-Lucent's R&D division.

TUGboat bibliography

A Chinese meta-font [**5**:2, November 1984]

A METAFONT-like system with PostScript output [**10**:4, December 1989]

Extending MetaPost: Response to "Even more MetaFun" [**21**:2, June 2000]

Drawing graphs with MetaPost [**22**:1-2, March/June 2001]

---

[1]The content of this introduction was drawn from John Hobby's TUG interview: `http://tug.org/interviews/hobby.html`

A METAFONT-like system with PostScript output

[Published in *TUGboat* **10**:4, December 1989]

Abstract The MetaPost system implements a language very much like METAFONT except that the output is expressed with cubic splines and PostScript commands rather than in METAFONT's raster-oriented Generic Font Format. It is a powerful language for expressing figures for documents printed on Postscript printers, and it can also be used for creating PostScript fonts.

The data types are mostly the same as in METAFONT, except that pictures represent a continuous version of what is scan-converted in order to create METAFONT's pictures. Some raster-oriented METAFONT primitives are removed and primitives for expressing PostScript concepts are added. Facilities are also included for adding text to pictures. This should make it convenient for figures to include labels that match the typography of the rest of the document.

1 Introduction

In addition to being a font-making tool, METAFONT is also a powerful graphics language. The only problem is that METAFONT produces raster output which is not very suitable for applications other than font making. This paper describes a tool for applying METAFONT's power as a graphics language to applications where PostScript output is more appropriate.

A less ambitious approach to the problem due to Leslie Carr had some success but ran into practical and theoretical difficulties [2]. Some work by Shimon Yanai avoids many of these problems by using a slightly altered version of METAFONT [7]. The work discussed here includes a number of important features that Yanai does not implement. It should avoid most of the difficulties encountered in earlier work, but one practical problem remains: PostScript character definitions based on METAFONT programs turn out to be rather large. Because of this, we concentrate on turning METAFONT into a system for typesetting graphics analogous to Brian Kernighan's pic [3,4].

Even with bitmap output, METAFONT has already found some use as a figure-drawing tool. METAFONT can be used to create a special font that contains one character for each figure in the document, and this font can be used to print all the figures. This works reasonably well for some output devices, but it does require working with characters that may be several inches wide. Another drawback is that it is difficult to create figures that contain text as well as graphics.

This paper describes a variant of METAFONT that is currently under development. The new system is called MetaPost. It processes a language very similar to METAFONT, but it produces PostScript programs instead of a gf file. The new output medium allows MetaPost to be used as a figure-drawing tool without dealing with enormous characters. It also facilitates MetaPost commands for integrating text and graphics.

MetaPost produces a sequence of PostScript programs that need to be merged with the rest of the document before being sent to a PostScript printer. If the document is written in TeX, then the dvi-to-PostScript translator should do the merging as indicated by Figure 1. If the TeX document uses downloaded fonts, then the translator must be modified to scan the included PostScript programs and ensure that any required characters get downloaded properly. Of course, the output of MetaPost will be designed to make this scanning process as easy as possible.

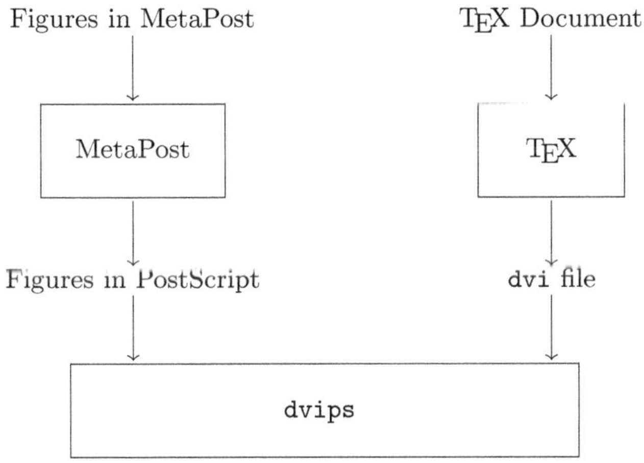

Fig. 1: A diagram of the processing for a TEX document with figures done in MetaPost.

The description of the language in Section 2 assumes familiarity with *The METAFONTbook* and concentrates on the differences between METAFONT and MetaPost.

Section 3 describes two possible extensions. The first is the use of a preprocessor to allow text included in MetaPost pictures to be coded in TEX. The second possible extension is a feature to allow resolution-dependent operations such as those that Knuth discusses in Chapter 24 of *The METAFONTbook* and uses in Computer Modern.

Finally, Section 4 contains a few concluding remarks.

2 The language

Since MetaPost is essentially an altered version of METAFONT, it is easiest to describe it by comparing it to METAFONT. We therefore assume some familiarity with METAFONT and describe the alterations necessary to deal with continuous rather than discrete output.

One important difference is that while METAFONT primitives work in units of pixels, MetaPost uses points, as TEX does. Since MetaPost is intended to be used with a macro package analogous to `plain.mf`, some of the differences in the primitives can be shielded from the user by suitable adjustments to the standard macro package.

2.1 Pens

Of METAFONT's eight data types, boolean, numeric, pair, path, string, and transform have no relation to the discrete raster and can be used in MetaPost as they are in METAFONT. The other two types are pen and picture. They both describe concepts that are useful in MetaPost, but their meaning is altered to eliminate their discrete flavor.

In the case of pens, this means that it is not appropriate for MetaPost to convert elliptical pens into polygons as METAFONT does[2] [5, pp. 148–149]. A better strategy for MetaPost is to treat elliptical pens as ideal ellipses so that appropriate PostScript

[2]Ideally. the Postscript interpreter should do this.

commands can be given when drawing with them. For example, in the case of a circular pen,

```
draw quartercircle scaled 200 withpen pencircle scaled 10
```

might be rendered in PostScript (Fig. 2) as

```
newpath
0 0 100 0 90 arc
10 setlinewidth 1 setlinecap stroke
```

Fig. 2: The result of a `draw` command with `pencircle scaled 10`

Using an elliptical pen of a more general shape,

```
draw quartercircle scaled 200 withpen pencircle xscaled 5 yscaled 10
```

can be rendered in Postscript (Fig. 3) as:

```
newpath
0 0 100 0 90 arc
1 2 scale
5 setlinewidth I setlinecap stroke
```

Fig. 3: The result of a `draw` command with `pencircle xscaled 5 yscaled 10`

METAFONT also allows polygonal pens to be constructed via the makepen operator or with the pensquare macro from `plain.mf`. MetaPost needs to treat such pens as polygons and implement them via PostScript's `fill` operator. For example,

```
draw quartercircle scaled 200 withpen pensquare scaled 10
```

might be rendered in PostScript (Fig. 4) as

```
newpath
105 -5 moveto
5 5 100 0 90 arc
-5 105 lineto
-5 -5 100 90 0 arcn
closepath fill
```

As explained in [6, part 241], METAFONT already implements drawing with polygonal pens by using the outline representation. MetaPost does the same thing except it turns the outline into PostScript commands instead of using it to control scan conversion routines.

Fig. 4: The result of a `draw` command with `pensquare scaled 10`

2.2 Pictures

The picture data type loses its discrete flavor in MetaPost, and this affects the set of operations allowed on pictures. MetaPost pictures function mainly as repositories for the results of draw commands and differ from METAFONT pictures in that they do not get digitized until after they have been translated into PostScript and read by the PostScript interpreter. Thus MetaPost does not have METAFONT's restriction on the types of transformations that can be applied to pictures (see [5, pp. 117, 144]). Another consequence of the non-discrete nature of MetaPost pictures is the loss of the `totalweight` operator.

One of the more fundamental differences between METAFONT pictures and MetaPost pictures is in how pixel values are interpreted. In a METAFONT picture, each pixel has a numeric weight, `draw` commands add to the weights, and pixels with positive weights are considered to be black. In contrast, MetaPost adopts PostScript's view of the world where pixels have colors and drawing operators assign new values to the colors of affected pixels. Thus while the `unfill` macro from `plain.mf` is implemented with the `cull` command. the analogous operation in MetaPost is accomplished by filling `withcolor white`.[3]

An important feature of MetaPost pictures is that they can contain textual labels. The text can come from any font for which there is a `tfm` file available, but the PostScript version of the picture assumes that the font is known to the printer and is scaled to match the design size in the `tfm` file. If the picture is to be included in a TeX document, then support code is needed in the dvi-to-PostScript translator in

[3] METAFONT's `cull` command is not implemented in MetaPost because it deals with pixel weights and therefore does not fit into PostScript's view of the world.

order to ensure that these conditions are satisfied.

The syntax for generating textual labels involves a single operator `infont`:

⟨picture secondary⟩ ⟶ ⟨string primary⟩ `infont` ⟨string primary⟩

This produces a picture that contains the given string set in the given font at the design size specified in the `tfm` file with the reference point of the first character at $(0,0)$. The result can then be transformed as desired and added to a picture variable, as in:

```
addto currentpicture also "label" infont "cmr10"
scaled 1.2 shifted (100,100)
```

Operators for finding the bounding box of a textual label facilitate placing the label and ensuring that there is enough space for it. This information is available to MetaPost from reading the `tfm` file and can be accessed via the following operators:

⟨pair primary⟩ ⟶ ⟨`llcorner` ⟨picture primary⟩
| `ulcorner` ⟨picture primary⟩
| `lrcorner` ⟨picture primary⟩
| `urcorner` ⟨picture primary⟩

These operators find the bounding box of any picture whether or not it is the result of `infont`. This includes all elements of the picture, even those filled `withcolor white`.

2.3 Drawing commands

Drawing commands in MetaPost must differ from those in METAFONT in order to take advantage of the features of PostScript, but the overall syntax is similar except for the new features. Thus MetaPost primitive commands has METAFONT's

`addto` ⟨picture variable⟩ `contour` ⟨path expression⟩ ⟨with list⟩
`addto` ⟨picture variable⟩ `doublepath` ⟨path expression⟩ ⟨with list⟩

and the corresponding macros

`fill` ⟨path expression⟩ ⟨with list⟩
`draw` ⟨path expression⟩ ⟨with list⟩

where a ⟨with list⟩ can be empty or contain various kinds of clauses. New kinds of clauses that provide access to PostScript features are explained below.

MetaPost interprets `addto` commands and `fill` and `draw` macros as assigning a new color to some region of a picture, and this region is determined according to PostScript's non-zero winding number rule [1, Section 4.6]. Since the `safefill` macro defined in *The METAFONTbook* uses the same rule, MetaPost behaves roughly as METAFONT would if all calls to the `fill` macros were replaced by calls to `safefill` (see [5, p. 121]).

If the ⟨with list⟩ contains a

`withpen` ⟨pen expression⟩

clause, then the affected region is enlarged to include everything swept out by the pen.

The color to be assigned to the affected region is given by a

`withcolor` ⟨color expression⟩

clause. For this purpose, there is a three-component numeric type color normally accessed via predefined constants `white`, `black`, `red`, `green`, and `blue`. Colors can be added together, multiplied by numeric constants or used in mediation expressions. For example:

`0.3black + 0.7white` and `0.7[black,white]`

are the same shade of gray. Of course red, green, and blue will seldom be used as long as most PostScript printers can only handle black and white or use halftoning to render shades of gray.

Another important feature of PostScript is the ability to draw dashed lines. This is accessed by giving a

`dashed` ⟨picture expression⟩

clause in a ⟨with list⟩ and using the picture expression to specify the pattern of dashes desired. For example, the picture

```
begingroup clearit;
  draw (0,0)..(6,0);
  draw (14,0)..(20,0);
currentpicture endgroup
```

illustrated in Figure 5a may be used in a dashed clause to specify the dash pattern in Figure 5b, created by laying copies of Figure 5a end to end.

Fig. 5a: A dash pattern

Fig. 5b: A line created five from copies of it

This dash pattern is specified by the PostScript command

`[12 8] 6 setdash`

In general, `dashed` ⟨picture expression⟩ means that the pattern of dashes is what would be produced by laying copies of ⟨picture expression⟩ end to end. This ignores features of (picture expression) such as color and line width since the only purpose is to tell MetaPost what argument to give to PostScript's `setdash` operator.

To provide access to PostScript's clip operator, there is a primitive drawing command

`clip` ⟨picture variable⟩ `to` ⟨path expression⟩

and a macro

`clipto` ⟨path expression⟩

equivalent to

`clip currentpicture to` ⟨path expression⟩

The region affected by the clip command is determined by the usual non-zero winding number rule: but instead of being filled with black or some other color, the clipping region is treated as a window. and all parts of the picture falling outside of the window are removed.

3 Possible extensions

The MetaPost language described in Section 2 is basically a version of METAFONT with raster-oriented features removed and features added to provide access to PostScript primitives. A heavy reliance on Knuth's public-domain code for METAFONT should make this project manageable. This section describes other features that might not be included in the initial version of the language because either they are difficult to implement or they require a substantial amount of external software.

3.1 TEX text in pictures

Section 2.2 described an `infont` operator that could be used to add textual labels to pictures. While this is fine for simple applications, it makes no provision for mathematical typesetting or even interword spaces. Thus words need to be positioned individually, and math formulas require piecing together many characters from different fonts in a complicated fashion.

These difficulties could be avoided by having a preprocessor that reads a MetaPost input file with TEX commands interspersed, and outputs an identical file with the TEX commands replaced by sequences of `addto` commands involving `infont` operations. This would produce an ordinary MetaPost input file that could then be processed in the usual way.

The preprocessor would work by running the interspersed commands through TEX and then extracting the character placement information from the dvi file. To find the picture expression corresponding o the TEX commands

```
$\displaystyle{\sqrt{3a+b\over ac}}$
```

the preprocessor could use TEX to obtain a dvi file containing this equation on a page by itself. The preprocessor could then scan the dvi file to find the coordinates of each character and each horizontal or vertical rule on the page. It is then a simple matter for the preprocessor to create an appropriate MetaPost picture expression. In the above example, this leads to the following picture expression:

```
def addalso = addto currentpicture also enddef;
begingroup
  save currentpicture;
  picture currentpicture;
  clearit;
  addalso "r" infont "cmex10" shifted (0,15.96);
  fill unitsquare xscaled 29.2 yscaled 0.4 shifted (10,15.96);
  addalso "3" infont "cmr10" shifted (11.2,6.77);
  addalso "a" infont "cmmi10 shifted (16.2,6.77);
  addalso "+" infont "cmr10" shifted (23.71,6.77);
  addalso "b" infont "cmmi10" shifted (33.71,6.77);
  fill unitsquare xscaled 26.8 yscaled 0.4 shifted (11.2,2.61)
  addalso "ac" infont "cmmi10" shifted (19.79,-6.86);
  currentpicture
endgroup
```

This MetaPost picture contains all the components of the formula exactly as TEX would typeset them, except that the horizontal rules have been replaced by calls to the fill macro. If the required fonts are available, the formula should look as though it were typeset by TEX except that it may be difficult to ensure that the rounding to pixel units is done according to the rules found in `dvitype`.

3.2 Pixel rounding

MetaPost has not been designed to deal with discrete pixels because its PostScript output is continuous in nature. However, the PostScript interpreter does produce pixel output and it may need help if it is to do a good job. In order to provide this help, a PostScript program occasionally needs to transform coordinates into what the PostScript manuals call device space to facilitate pixel-oriented rounding operations.

Techniques for coping with discreteness are discussed in Chapter 24 of *The METAFONTbook*. Since many of them are specific to font making, they are most applicable when MetaPost is being used to create a PostScript font. As Leslie Carr concluded in [2], this seems to be impractical at present because of the large size of a PostScript font description. However, this problem might be alleviated by future advances in PostScript interpreters combined with techniques for simplifying the character descriptions by degrading the outlines slightly.

Regardless of the application, it is worth considering how to implement something like the round macro from `plain.mf`. When applied to a pair, the round macro finds the nearest pixel corner. The following PostScript commands perform the same operation on a coordinate pair at the top of the operand stack:

```
itransform round exch round exch transform
```

The problem in using this is that MetaPost would not know the value of the pair computed by the round macro. All it would have would be a string of PostScript commands for computing it. Thus all subsequent operations involving the pair would also have be maintained as sequences of PostScript commands. For instance, the result of

```
round(3,2) + (4,1)
```

might be the following PostScript commands:

```
3 2 itransform round exch round exch transform
1 add exch 4 add exch
```

Note that the coordinates (3,2) and (4,1) are in units of points, not pixels.

Not all operations on a pair such as `round(3,2)` can easily be done in PostScript. For example, in a path expression such as

`round(3,2)`⟨up⟩`..(7,3)`

MetaPost computes control points according to the rules on pages 130–132 of *The METAFONTbook*. Rather than attempt to do this with PostScript commands, it seems more natural to start by converting

`(3,2)`⟨up⟩`..(7,3)`

into

(3.2)..controls (3.4.2122) and (5.95897,4.95193)..(7.3)

as usual. It is then a relatively simple matter to give PostScript commands that compute control points near (3,4.2122) and (5.95897,4.95193) based on the assumption that the curve begins at the rounded version of (3,2).

Generalizing from this example, it would be nice to be able to specify a PostScript procedure and a MetaPost macro that computes an approximation. For the above example, the PostScript procedure is

```
itransform round exch round exch transform
```

and the MetaPost macro is

```
def round primary p = p enddef
```

Although in this case the macro operates on a pair and returns a pair, the basic idea works for other combinations of types. The only requirement is that the arguments and results be of types that can be manipulated in PostScript. There is no formal requirement about how well the result of the MetaPost macro should approximate the result of the PostScript procedure. It just needs to be good enough to achieve reasonable results when used for things like path construction. Anything comparable to the half-pixel accuracy in the above example should be sufficient.

It remains to be tested in practice, but it seems very promising to be able to delay some computations until the PostScript interpreter is run on MetaPost's output. It would certainly be very flexible and would impose no hard and fast limitations on the techniques to be used to cope with the discreteness of the pixel grid.

4 Conclusion

We have outlined a language based on METAFONT with modifications to make it more suited to PostScript output. Except for the extensions discussed in Section 3, the implementation should be a relatively straightforward modification to the public domain code for METAFONT. The language is designed for generating graphics such as figures for technical papers, but it could be used for almost any application involving graphics and the generation of PostScript programs. Because the language is so much like METAFONT at the user level, it is tempting to consider taking existing METAFONT programs for a typeface such as Computer Modern and rewriting some of the macros so that the programs could be processed by MetaPost.

References

[1] Adobe Systems Incorporated. *PostScript Language Reference Manual.* Reading, Mass.: Addison-Wesley, 1986.

[2] Carr, Leslie. "Of METAFONT and PostScript." TEXniques 5:141–152. 1988.

[3] Kernighan, Brian W. "PIC — A Language for Typesetting Graphics." *Software Practice and Experience 12*(1):1–21, 1982.

[4] Kernighan, Brian W. *PIC — A Graphics Language for Typesetting. Computing Science Technical Report* 116. Murray Hill, New Jersey: AT&T Bell Laboratories, 1984.

[5] Knuth, Donald E. *The METAFONTbook.* Reading, Mass.: Addison-Wesley, 1984.

[6] Knuth, Donald E. *METAFONT: The Program. Computers and Typesetting*, Vol. D. Reading, Mass.: Addison-Wesley, 1986.

[7] Yanai, Shimon. *Environment for Translating METAFONT to PostScript.* M.Sc. Thesis. Faculty of Computer Science, Technion: Haifa, Israel, 1989.

One Picture is Worth Ten Thousand Words.
— FRED R. BARNARD, *Printers' Ink* (1927)

People who gush that a picture is worth 1,000 words
usually fail to point out that it may well take
a million computer "words" to send or store it.
— ROBERT LUCKY, *Silicon Dreams* (1993)

TUG 2001
A
TEX
Odyssey
DELAWARE OR BUST

7
Frank Liang

By 1977 Franklin Liang was already involved with Donald Knuth and TEX. According to the Acknowledgements in his thesis (`http://tug.org/docs/liang`), Frank began his involvement with TEX as a summer job. In Frank's paper reproduced in this chapter, he states that the hyphenation algorithm described in the paper "was developed by Prof. Knuth and myself in the summer of 1977." We also know that in the summer of 1977 Donald Knuth revised `TEXDR.AFT` [*Digital Typography*, pp. 481–504] to be `TEX.ONE` [*Digital Typography*, pp. 505–532] so his research assistants Frank Liang and Michael Plass could prepare a prototype implementation while he was away on a trip.

The original implementation of hyphenation in TEX was changed for TEX82, using the pattern-based method hinted at in the final short section of the paper reproduced here, which was also the subject of Frank's thesis dated August 1983. This method is also described in Appendix H of *The TEXbook*.

We also know that during his time at Stanford, Frank did some other mathematical work: "A Lower Bound for On-Line Bin Packing," *Information Processing Letters 10*(2), pp. 76–79, 1980; *The Dinner Table Problem* (with Bengt Aspvall, `ftp://db.stanford.edu/pub/cstr.old/reports/cs/tr/80/829/CS-TR-80-829.pdf`). In any case, Frank's pattern-based method for hyphenation is essentially statistical. In 1979 Frank was a teaching assistant for Knuth's Concrete Mathematics course which was given that year by Ron Graham.

Frank's pattern-based approach to hyphenation essentially solved the hyphenation problem for TEX and has been used in many other free software document processors, such as OpenOffice and Apache FOP. (The method may also be used in various commercial systems.) A 2007 document on *troff* (`http://heirloom.sourceforge.net/doctools/troff.pdf`) credits Frank's approach to hyphenation.

By now, sets of patterns have been produced for essentially all languages that use hyphenation (see, for instance, `http://ctan.org/tex-archive/language/hyph-utf8`).

TUGboat bibliography: The paper included here is Frank's only item in *TUGboat*.

TEX and hyphenation

[Published in *TUGboat* **2**:2, July 1981]

Word hyphenation is a useful feature of any computerized document formatting system. Sometimes it is also one of the most embarrassing.*

The current hyphenation algorithm was developed by Prof. Knuth and myself in the summer of 1977. Our goal was to come up with a reasonably compact algorithm that would find a significant percentage of possible hyphenation points, but would make very few errors. The algorithm is described in Appendix H of the TEX manual. Note that there have been quite a few minor changes since the original printing of the manual; these are described in the errata file.

Basically, the algorithm has four types of rules: (1) Prefix removal (e.g. `com-`, `dis-`, `ex-`), (2) Suffix removal (e.g. `-able`, `-ful`, `-tion`), (3) Vowel-consonant-consonant-vowel rule (can usually split between the consonants), and (4) Exception table (about 300 entries). Actually, these parts are applied in the order (4), (2), (1), (3); this order is rather important because of the interaction between rules. For example, the `horse-` prefix was put in not so much because we were concerned about hyphenating words like `horse-power` correctly, but rather to avoid hyphenating them incorrectly (the vccv rule (3) would break `hor-sepower`).

The rules were mostly found by hand. Good prefixes were found by looking through a dictionary; suffixes by looking through a reverse dictionary. Other ad hoc rules were discovered as the development proceeded (break vowel-q, break after ck). However, as good computer scientists, we then used an on-line copy of the American Heritage Dictionary (at Xerox PARC) to test our rules. This testing had two purposes: (1) to determine which pairs of consonants should be split under the vccv rule, and (2) to generate a list of exceptions to the rules. The exception list originally contained thousands of words, but was pruned down to just a few hundred. Also, in some cases new rules were formulated to take care of large classes of exceptions.

How well does the algorithm work in practice? Quite well, it seems. Quantitatively, in a test on a pocket dictionary word list, the algorithm found about 40% of the allowable hyphen points, with about 1% in error. Furthermore, the hyphen points found were usually the most reasonable or "good" places to break the word. In practice, the algorithm almost never makes a glaring mistake, while at the same time the user does not very often need to specify explicit (discretionary) hyphens, unless the columns are very narrow (or letters very wide).

The algorithm takes about 4K 36-bit words of code, including the exception dictionary.

A note on the implementation: If the algorithm is programmed by sequentially checking each of the rules to see if it applies, it will run rather slowly. Using a hash table would improve things,, but a faster and more compact way is to use a version of a finite state machine. Interested readers should look at the actual code.

Time magazine algorithm

This is reputedly the most widely used hyphenation algorithm (of acceptable quality). The idea is to decide whether or not to split a word based on four letters `wx-yz`

*If you find any such embarrassing hyphenations done by TEX, you are encouraged to send them to the author.

around the potential hyphen point. However, this would require storing a table of $26^2 = 456,976$ bits, which is excessive. (Actually, only about 10-15% of these 4-letter patterns actually occur in English words, but it seems the storage would still be considerable.)

Instead, the algorithm uses three tables of size $26^2 = 676$, corresponding to the pairs `wx`, `xy`, and `yz`. The origin of these tables seems to have been forgotten, but they are supposed to represent the conditional probability of a break given that the first two, middle two, or last two letters, respectively, are a particular pair. To decide whether to break at a given point, the values for the three pairs are looked up, multiplied together (as if they were independent probabilities, which they are not), and then compared to a threshold.

Adjusting the threshold obviously changes the performance of the algorithm. One estimate is: 40% hyphens found with 10% error. In any case a large exception dictionary will be required for good performance. One reason for this is that looking at just four letters around the potential hyphen point is not sufficient. The author has discovered examples where one must look as much as 7 letters ahead (!) to determine hyphenation (consider `def-i-ni-tion` vs. `de-fin-i-tive`).

Patterns

Currently the TEX project (more precisely, me) is conducting research into better hyphenation algorithms. In particular, I am investigating a method based on the idea of hyphenating and inhibiting patterns. For example, a hyphenating pattern might be `-tion`, indicating that whenever tion occurs in a word, we can hyphenate immediately before it. Another good example is `c-c`. Note that hyphenating patterns are a generalization of the prefix, suffix, and vccv rules discussed above.

In addition, the idea of inhibiting rules has proved useful. Such rules formalize the notion of "we can usually hyphenate such and such a pattern, except when it is followed by ...". Also, such rules are often useful for handling classes of exceptions.

More importantly, we hope to be able to extract the rules automatically from an on-line dictionary. This will be done by collecting statistics on the effectiveness of all possible patterns, and then using some heuristics to choose a good set of patterns. Preliminary experiments with this approach indicate that it will be very effective. For example, a set of about 3300 hyphenating and 2700 inhibiting patterns gets 85% of the hyphens with 2% error.

The hyphenation algorithm we have now was Frank Liang's Ph.D. research.
He worked with me on the original hyphenation method,
and his experience led him to discover a much better way,
which can adapt to all languages—
I mean to all western languages, which are the languages that use hyphens.

—DONALD KNUTH, *Digital Typography* (1999)

This exercise takes awhile,
but the data structures are expecially interesting;
the hyphenation algorithm is a nice little part of the program
that can be studied in isolation.

—DONALD KNUTH, *TUGboat* (1990)

8
Oren Patashnik

Oren Patashnik was born and raised in the Seattle area, graduating from Redmond High School. He attended college at Yale, graduating in 1976 in mathematics and computer science.

Oren remained in New Haven during the following year finishing his proof that Qubic (4x4x4 tic-tac-toe) was, under optimal play, a win for the first player.

To support himself that year, Oren worked as a research assistant with some experimental psychologists, and the following year wound up at Bell Labs, also working with an experimental psychologist. He spent three more years at Bell Labs before starting graduate school. At Bell Labs he also met Ron Graham.

Oren started graduate school in computer science at Stanford in the fall of 1980. For the first several years, he had research assistantships arranged through Donald Knuth. Oren was also a teaching assistant for Ron Graham when Graham taught the "Concrete Mathematics" course at Stanford in the fall of 1981, and again in 1984 with Knuth teaching the course. Both times involved writing up a full set of class notes.

Owen recalls that Graham and Knuth had been planning a book based on the Concrete Mathematics course and they asked him to synthesize a first-pass book draft based on all the years of class notes. Over several years starting around 1983, he did produce the first draft and, thus, became a co-author with Graham and Knuth when the book was published in 1988.

In late 1982, Leslie Lamport was looking for someone to do a bibliography support program for LaTeX — Oren recalls it being described as "a 3-week project." Thus he started work on what became BibTeX. He finished a preliminary version in about 1984, and the first public release was in 1985 (BibTeX 0.89). The second release (0.99) came out in 1985, and a stable version was released after the "BibTeX 1.0" paper was published (see bibliography below). This year (2010), he has restarted work on BibTeX, and has already made one small bug-fix release.

Oren finished his doctorate in computer science in 1990 with the thesis topic of *Optimal Circuit Segmentation for Pseudo-Exhaustive Testing.*

Since Stanford, Oren has been a researcher at the Center for Communications Research, La Jolla.

TUGboat bibliography

BibTeX 1.0 [**15**:3, September 1994]

BibTeX 101 [**19**:2, June 1998]

BibTeX yesterday, today, and tomorrow [**24**:1, 2003]

BIBTEX 101

[Published in *TUGboat* **19**:2, June 1998]

Abstract This paper introduces BIBTEX to those having little or no previous BIBTEX experience but having at least some familiarity with TEX or LATEX. It also answers some frequently asked BIBTEX questions, from complete novices as well as from experienced users.

Introduction

BIBTEX is the bibliography program designed originally to accompany Leslie Lamport's LATEX; it now works with other incarnations of TEX, too. BIBTEX removes the tedium, and adds some flexibility, in producing a reference list.[1] When BIBTEX creates your reference list, it's BIBTEX, not you, minding the minutiae like ensuring that your reference-list entries are in the correct order, that every comma is in place, and that the information is formatted consistently across entries. Furthermore, a single, simple, change of bibliography-style name lets you convert your reference list from style A (which might order the entries alphabetically, spell out journal names in full, and list all authors as first-name then last-name), to a completely different style B (which might order the entries according to their order of mention in the text, abbreviate journal names, and invert just the first author's first and last names).

The next section of the paper explains how to use BIBTEX. The final section answers some frequently asked BIBTEX questions.

Getting started with BIBTEX

To use BIBTEX, you first put your bibliographic information into a bibliography database file. For example, your file `mybib.bib` (all database file names end with `.bib`) might contain an entry like:

```
@BOOK{knuth:tex,
  author = "Donald E. Knuth",
  title = "The {{\TeX}}book",
  publisher = "Addison-Wesley",
  year = 1984,
}
```

The `@BOOK` tells BIBTEX that this is a book entry type. The `knuth:tex` is the database key, which is a sequence of characters to be used as the name for this entry. And the rest of the entry comprises four ⟨field⟩ = ⟨field-value⟩ pairs appropriate for a `BOOK` entry type. In general you will have many such entries in a database file; you might also have multiple database files.

Once you've entered the bibliographic information into the database file(s), the hard part is done. For the easy part, you put into your (LA)TEX[2] source file citations like

```
... in the \TeX{}book~\cite{knuth:tex} ...
```

[1]Throughout this paper, the term 'reference list' is used generally to refer to what might also be called a 'bibliography' or a 'list of sources' or anything similar.

[2]The term '(LA)TEX' is used to mean either LATEX or plain (or other variations of) TEX.

The \cite command's argument here, knuth:tex, is called a cite-key, and must match the corresponding database-key. (LA)TEX might typeset this \cite command as

... in the TEXbook [23] ... or

... in the TEXbook[23] ... or

... in the TEXbook (Knuth, 1984) ...

depending on the citation style. (LA)TEX's default citation style uses a number in brackets, and for that citation style, together with an appropriate bibliography style, the corresponding reference-list entry might look like:

23. Donald E. Knuth. *The TEXbook.* Addison-Wesley, 1984.

Besides the citation commands, you also put into your (LA)TEX source file two BIBTEX-related commands:

```
\bibliography{mybib}
\bibliographystyle{plain}
```

The \bibliography command does two things; it tells (LA)TEX to put the reference list at that spot in your document, and it tells BIBTEX which file(s) to use for the bibliographic database, here just the single file mybib.bib. The \bibliographystyle command tells (LA)TEX nothing, but tells BIBTEX which bibliography style to use, here the standard style plain; bibliography style file names end with .bst, thus the relevant file is plain.bst in this case.

So with your database file(s) and your (LA)TEX source file structured appropriately, your citations are formatted according to the citation style, and your reference list is formatted according to the bibliography style.

To actually produce the typeset document, you run (LA)TEX, BIBTEX, (LA)TEX, (LA)TEX. The first (LA)TEX run writes, to an .aux file, information for use by BIBTEX— which bibliography style to use, which database file(s) to use, and which database entries to include. The BIBTEX run reads all that information from the .aux file, reads the specified database (.bib) file(s), formats the reference list according to the instructions in the bibliography style (.bst) file, and writes its output onto a .bbl file. The next (LA)TEX run reads the .bbl file and incorporates the reference list into the document. The final (LA)TEX run fixes the references into the reference list. Figure 8.1 shows the files that BIBTEX uses. The .blg file is BIBTEX's log file, in which BIBTEX records any warning or error messages.

To try using BIBTEX with LATEX, put the six-line BOOK entry shown on the previous page into a file called mybib.bib, and then, into a file called mypaper1.tex, put these six lines of LATEX:

```
\documentclass{article}
\begin{document}
The \TeX{}book~\cite{knuth:tex} is good.
\bibliography{mybib}
\bibliographystyle{plain}
\end{document}
```

Exactly how you run LATEX and BIBTEX is system-dependent, but on my system I type four commands:

```
latex mypaper1
bibtex mypaper1
latex mypaper1
latex mypaper1
```

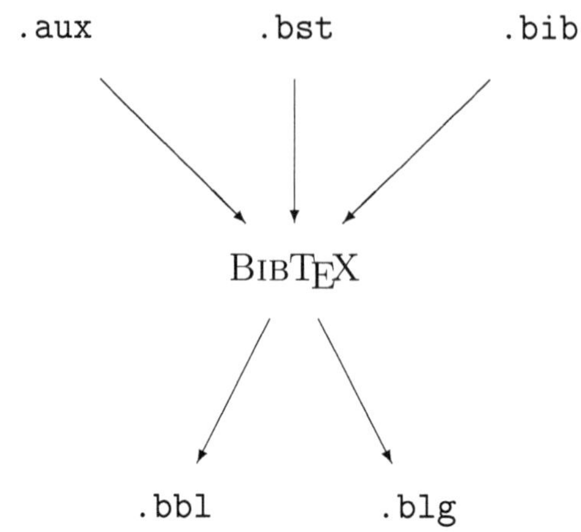

Figure 8.1: BibTeX's input and output files.

To try using BibTeX with plain TeX, create the file `mybib.bib` as above, and then put into a file called `mypaper2.tex` these seven lines of plain TeX:

```
\input btxmac
The \TeX{}book~\cite{knuth:tex} is good.
\medskip
\leftline{\bf References}
\bibliography{mybib}
\bibliographystyle{plain}
\bye
```

To run `mypaper2` through TeX and BibTeX on my system I simply type

```
tex mypaper2
bibtex mypaper2
tex mypaper2
tex mypaper2
```

But `mypaper2` `\input`s the file `btxmac.tex`, which contains the macros that make BibTeX work with plain TeX. Those macros are a standard part of most TeX distributions, but if they're not a part of yours, you'll have to go fetch a copy from CTAN in `tex-archive/macros/plain/contrib/`.

That's a brief introduction to BibTeX. The following sources provide further details. Leslie Lamport's LaTeX manual [3] explains how to use BibTeX with LaTeX. In particular, section B.1 describes the `.bib`-file format in detail. The file `btxmac.tex` [1] documents its own use, with or without Karl Berry's `eplain.tex` package (for which the `btxmac` macros were originally written). The "BibTeXing" document [4], which is distributed along with BibTeX itself, contains further hints for BibTeX users. The "Designing BibTeX Styles" document [5], also distributed with BibTeX, explains the postfix stack-based language used to write BibTeX bibliography styles (`.bst`) files. *The LaTeX Companion* [2], by Michel Goossens, Frank Mittelbach, and Alexander Samarin, summarizes much of the information contained in the sources above, and it describes some of the tools available for helping with BibTeX bibliographies. Norman Walsh's *Making TeX Work* [7] also describes such tools. (Many users find the tools for managing bibliographic database files to be particularly useful.) BibTeX's standard bibliography styles, like `plain`, are based on Mary-Claire van Leunen's *A Handbook for Scholars* [6]. That book is worthwhile reading for anyone wanting to design a bibliography style.

Frequently Asked BIBTEX Questions (FABQs)

The questions in this section are ordered, roughly, by user sophistication, with the earlier questions coming from the least experienced users.

FABQ: Can I include an entry in the reference list without having to give an in-text citation for it?

Answer: Yes. If there's a `\nocite{my-ref}` in your (LA)TEX source file, the entry whose database-key is `my-ref` will appear in the reference list but without a corresponding in-text citation.

FABQ: Can I include all the entries in my database in the reference list without my having to `\cite` or `\nocite` all of them explicitly?

Answer: Yes. Putting a `\nocite{*}` command in your (LA)TEX source file has the effect of putting in that spot of your source file a `\nocite` command for each entry in your database.

FABQ: If I can't find a bibliography style to my liking, how can I make my own bibliography style (`.bst`) file?

Answer: The `.bst` language is fairly flexible, but it's meant to be programmed, except for simple changes, by reasonably experienced programmers. Patrick Daly's `custom-bib/makebst` package, on the other hand, allows nonprogrammers, too, to create their own bibliography styles.

FABQ: How can I have two different database files use the same set of abbreviations without duplicating the abbreviations?

Answer: If you put all your abbreviations, like

```
@STRING{A-W = "Addison-Wesley"}
```

into a database file, say `abrvs.bib`, containing just abbreviations, and if you list that file first in the `\bibliography` command, then all other `.bib` files listed in that command may use the abbreviations in `abrvs.bib`. For example, two files `cs-books.bib` and `math-books.bib` may have entries that use the field

```
publisher = A-W,
```

if the `\bibliography` command looks like

```
\bibliography{abrvs,cs-books,math-books}
```

FABQ: How can I keep BIBTEX from converting all my journal-article titles to lower case?

Answer: Technically, it's the bibliography style file, not BIBTEX itself, that's doing the case conversion. Many bibliography styles (*The Chicago Manual of Style*, for example) say that a reference-list entry for a journal article should have the article title converted to lower case, because it is a smaller thing inside a bigger thing, but should have the title of the bigger thing — the journal title itself — left in uppers-and-lowers form (in which you capitalize the first word, and, in most styles, the first word after a colon — which indicates a subtitle — and all other words except articles and unstressed conjunctions and prepositions). But if you don't like that style, it's a simple change to the `.bst` file to eliminate the case conversion. For example, many `.bst` files will have something like:

```
FUNCTION {format.title}
{ title empty$
    { "" }
    { title "t" change.case$ }
  if$
}
```

That's the function that converts the titles of, for example, journal articles, from uppers-and-lowers form to lowercase. Changing that function to

```
FUNCTION {format.title}
{ title field.or.null
}
```

will eliminate the case conversion.

FABQ: How can I change the citations from using brackets to using parentheses or superscripts?

Answer: Certain bibliography style (`.bst`) files have accompanying (LA)TEX style files; make sure you are using the accompanying (LA)TEX style file if it's required. For example, if you are using the `apalike` bibliography and citation style, which uses parentheses rather than brackets in its citations, you need, in addition to `apalike.bst`, either `apalike.sty` (under LATEX) or `apalike.tex` (under plain TEX). You invoke those files with a

```
\usepackage{apalike}
```

command under LATEX, or a

```
\input apalike
```

command under plain TEX. If there is no such accompanying (LA)TEX style file for your `.bst` file, you must redefine `\cite` and any other relevant citation command yourself.

FABQ: Sometimes I enter an author in my database file as

```
author = "D.E. Knuth",
```

but in my reference list the author appears without the middle initial, as just 'D. Knuth'—what's going on?

Answer: Probably you are using a bibliography style that automatically abbreviates first names to just initials. In this case, BIBTEX thinks that 'D.E.' is a single name, rather than two initials, because there is no space between the initials, and the style abbreviates this to 'D.' The solution is to, in the database file, insert a space between the initials:

```
author = "D. E. Knuth",
```

If you really want to close up the space between initials in the output, it's a simple matter to change the bibliography style file to do that.

FABQ: How can I have other BIBTEX questions answered?

Answer: Post them to the `comp.text.tex` newsgroup; I've been known to send private email replies to questions that seem to receive inadequate answers in that newsgroup.

References

[1] Karl Berry and Oren Patashnik. `btxmac.tex`. Macros to make BIBTEX work with plain TEX; current version 0.99k, 13 November 1995.

[2] Michel Goossens, Frank Mittelbach, and Alexander Samarin. *The LATEX Companion.* Addison-Wesley, 1994.

[3] Leslie Lamport. *LATEX: A Document Preparation System.* Addison-Wesley, second edition, 1994.

[4] Oren Patashnik. BIBTEXing. General documentation for BIBTEX users, contained in the file `btxdoc.tex`, 8 February 1988.

[5] Oren Patashnik. Designing BIBTEX styles. Documentation for BIBTEX style dosignors, containod in tho filo `btxhak.tox`, 8 Fobruary 1088.

[6] Mary-Claire van Leunen. *A Handbook for Scholars.* Oxford University Press, revised edition, 1992.

[7] Norman Walsh. Making TEX Work. O'Reilly & Associates, 103 Morris Street, Suite A, Sebastopol, CA 95472, 1994.

Various organizations and individuals have developed
BIBTEX style files that correspond to the house style
of particular journals or editing houses.
Nelson Beebe has collected
a large number of BIBTEX styles.

— FRANK MITTELBACH et al., *The LATEX Companion Second Edition* (2004)

```
@UNPUBLISHED{btxdoc,
 author = "Oren Patashnik",
 title = "{{\BibTeX ing}}",
 note = "Documentation for general {\BibTeX} users",
 month = "8~" # feb,
 year = 1988 }
```

— OREN PATASHNIK, *BIBTEXing* (1988)

9

Michael Plass

After they obtained MS degrees from Northern Illinois University, Michael Plass and his wife Susan[1] moved to California where Michael attended Stanford. In his first semester at Stanford, Michael had Donald Knuth as his professor for a course where one of the assignments involved open-ended problems, including the line-breaking problem.

The following summer (1977) Knuth revised `TEXDR.AFT` [*Digital Typography*, pp. 481–504] to be `TEX.ONE` [*Digital Typography*, pp. 505–532] so his research assistants Michael Plass and Frank Liang could prepare a prototype implementation while he was away on a trip.

Michael has recalled,[2]

> Frank worked on the output modules, and I worked on the allocator, parser, macro processor, and so forth. On August 24, we combined our programs, and after a bit of debugging, were able to process a subset of TEX input all the way to XGP output. Knuth, on his return from China, seemed pleased with our efforts, and proceeded to re-code TEX himself. He asked me to continue to work out details of the line-breaking.

Later, when Michael was looking for a thesis topic, he returned to[3]

> the line-breaking problem and extended it to the problem of pagination, taking into account floating figures.[4]

Michael's thesis was one of the first to be typeset in TEX.

Michael's approach to line-breaking also essentially solved the problem once and for all for TEX and has been copied by many other document processing systems.

After Stanford, Michael moved to Xerox Palo Alto Research Center where he has remained ever since, mostly working with graphics and printing.

TUGboat bibliography: The paper included here is Michael's only item in *TUGboat*.

Editor's note: TEX as discussed in this paper is TEX78. Rather trying to recompile this paper with TEX78, we scanned and incorporated the figures as originally printed in *TUGboat*. However, see also the additional editor's note at the end of the paper.

---

[1]Susan has also been involved with TEX, as a member of the TUG board and an author for *TUGboat*: `http://tug.org/TUGboat/Contents/listauthor.html#Plass,Susan`

[2]TUG Interview Corner, `http://tug.org/interviews/plass.html`

[3]Ibid.

[4]*Optimal Pagination Techniques for Automatic Typesetting*, `http://tug.org/docs/plass/`

Charting your grammar with TEX

[Published in *TUGboat* **2**:3, November 1981]

Are you one of those people who would rather look at a syntax chart than a BNF grammar? Do you avoid making a syntax chart for your language because it is too hard to draw or too hard to typeset? If so, this is the article for you. Pay attention, and you will learn how to use the macros below to create your own syntax charts with TEX.

First some basics. Every component of the syntax chart is enclosed in a TEX box, with the entry and exit points on the left and right sides of the box, aligned with the baseline. Usually the entry point is on the left end and the exit is on the right, but not always, as we shall see.

The simplest components are the boxes that represent the terminals and the nonterminals of the language. The terminals are the lowest level pieces of the language that the description deals with, for example, keywords, special characters, letters, digits, and so forth. Nonterminals are the names for the building blocks of the language. Some examples of nonterminal symbols might be number, identifier, expression, statement, program. If you are familiar with BNF, the nonterminals are the things in the angle brackets.

The terminals in a syntax chart are enclosed in boxes with rounded ends, and nonterminals are enclosed in rectangular boxes. This is how you use the syntax chart macros to make both kinds of elementary boxes:

`\Terminal{procedure}` ⇒ 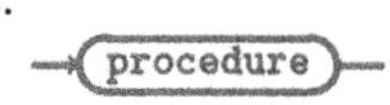

`\Nonterminal{statement}` ⇒ 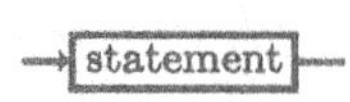

(Keep in mind that the case of the first letter in a TEX control sequence is significant.) You can control what fonts are used inside these boxes by defining the control sequences `\TerminalFont` and `\NonterminalFont` to be the appropriate font selectors. Notice each of these basic boxes have 'stems' on the left and right sides, one of them being an arrow and the other one just a line. TEX will determine which direction to point the arrow in on the basis of how the box is nested inside of other constructions.

The definition of a nonterminal is specified like this:

```
\Define{Letter A}\Terminal{A}\EndDef
```

⇒ 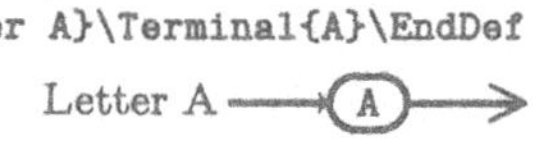

More complicated charts are built up by means of *sequencing*, *alternation*, and *repetition* of simpler charts. To illustrate the way these work, we will assume that the control sequence `\one` has been defined to be `\Nonterminal{one}`, and so forth.

Sequencing is easy to do; just put the subcharts together:

`\one\two\three` ⇒ 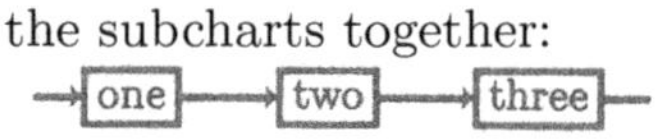

Alternation is a bit more complicated to specify. Here is an example:

```
\Alternatives
 {\Upper{\one}
  \Middle{\two}
  \Lower{\three}
  \Lower{\four}}
```

⇒ 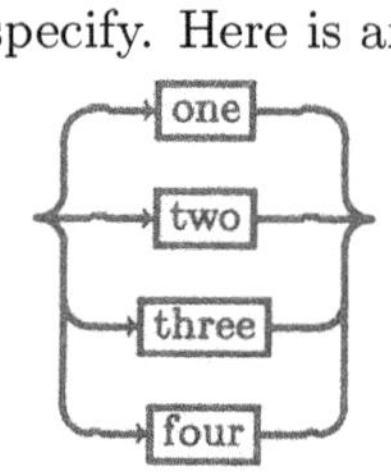

There may be any positive number of choices listed as the argument to `\Alternatives`, and each choice is marked by enclosing it in braces and preceding it with `\Upper`, `\Middle`, or `\Lower`. Things marked with `\Upper` go above the baseline, things marked with `\Lower` go below the baseline, and something marked with `\Middle` goes on the baseline. It is permitted to omit any one of these three kinds of tags:

```
\Alternatives
 {\Middle{\one}
  \Lower{\two}
  \Lower{\three}}
```

⇒

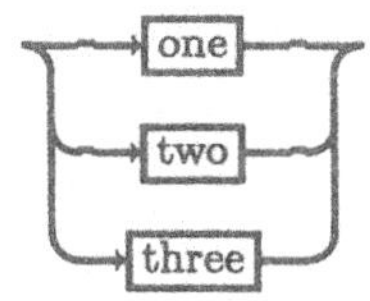

```
\Alternatives
 {\Upper{\one}
  \Upper{\two}
  \Lower{\three}}
```

⇒

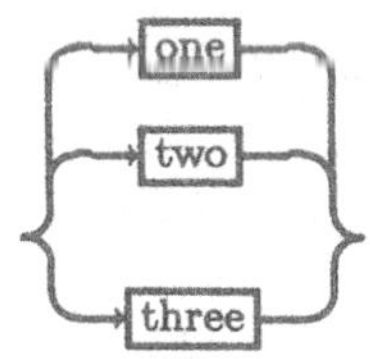

```
\Alternatives
 {\Upper{\one}
  \Upper{\two}
  \Middle{\three}}
```

⇒

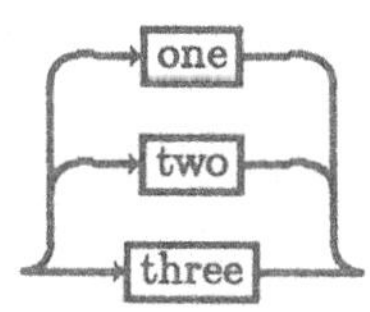

Sometimes a stack of alternatives can get very tall; in this case it might be better to spread them out horizontally:

```
\HorzAlternatives{\Alternative{\one}
 \Alternative{\two}\Alternative{\three}}
```

⇒

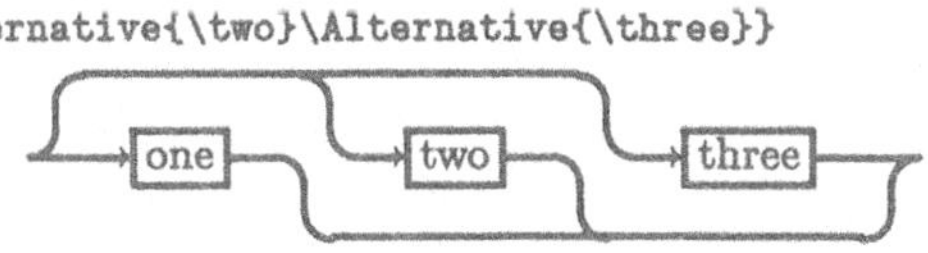

This one is especially appropriate for a long list of short choices.

Repetition is specified in almost exactly the same way as alternatives:

```
\Repeat{\Upper{\one}
        \Middle{\two}
        \Lower{\three}}
```

⇒

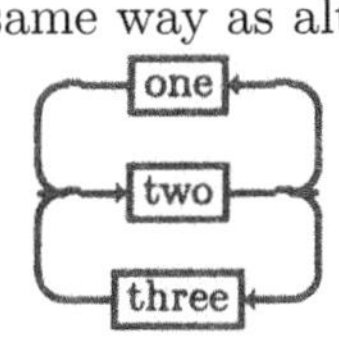

The same rules apply as before, except that you are not allowed to leave out the `\Middle`. This is not the same as specifying an empty middle, which you might often want to do:

```
\Repeat{\Upper{\one}\Middle{}}
```

⇒

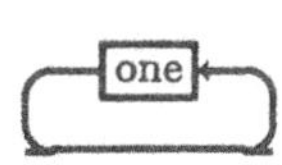

```
\Repeat{\Middle{\one}\Lower{}}
```

⇒

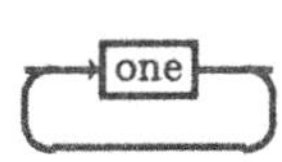

Sometimes a chart gets too wide for the page, and TeX breaks it up into lines as if it were a paragraph. If this is want you want, fine—but if you are in unrestricted horizontal mode, you can make a nicer transition to a new line by using `\NewLine`. Look at Appendix B for examples of this.

Now you know about all of the constructions. They can be nested in any way you please, up to a depth of four. One way to get around this limit is to save away the innermost parts of the diagram in a box and call it in when you need it. You can say `\AllocBox\cntrlseq` to define `\cntrlseq` to be a digit indicating a box that you can use; this way your box usage won't conflict with that of the syntax chart macros. Remember to use braces to enclose the section in which you use `\AllocBox`, so that the box number can be used again. If you exceed TeX's `varsize` limit, the usual solution is to force a page eject so TeX does not have to keep so much stuff in its memory.

To use the macros, say

```
\input SynChart
```

near the beginning of your file. When you actually want to make a chart, say `\SyntaxChart` to set up the baselineskip, lineskip, and some other stuff. If you are mixing syntax charts with other text, you will want to enclose the `\SyntaxChart` along with the chart definition in braces, so all the funny definitions go away at the end of the group and don't mess up the rest of your document. You will probably also want to say `\parindent 0pt` to eliminate the paragraph indentation.

The call on `\SyntaxChart` also tells TeX to ignore tabs and carriage returns so you can format your chart more easily. Just be careful where you add spaces — after a control sequence is OK, but not between or after the parameters to a macro. The reason for not ignoring spaces is so terminals and nonterminals can have embedded spaces; if you prefer, you can say `\IgnoreWhiteSpace` to cause spaces to be ignored too, and then put in a control-space where you really want a space.

Now would be a good time to go try making your own simple syntax chart, using the macro definitions in Appendix A. When defining a complex diagram, it is often helpful to first define pieces of it as TeX macros. This makes the source much easier to read, and keeps the nesting of braces down to a reasonable level. This device is used extensively in the example in Appendix B.

Finally, some fine points about spacing. The horizontal lines are actually composed of fixed-width rules and leaders filled with rules. The control sequence `\QLine` defines a fairly short fixed-width line, and `\QQLine` defines one twice as long. `\Fil` defines a line that stretches like glue, with a normal width of zero and the same stretchability as `\hfil`; `\Fill` is similar, but with the stretchability of an `\hfill`. Each component of a repetition or (vertical) alternation construction implicitly has `\Fil` on each side, so if the components are not all the same width, the available space in each of the shorter ones will be distributed evenly between the embedded `\Fil`s and the ends of the component. By using these macros in various combinations, you can get any kind of horizontal spacing you want.

When a terminal box contains only special character or only upper case letters, the result looks best when the contents are centered vertically in the box; this is the default. However, if the same thing is done for lower case letters, the baselines of the words in different boxes may not line up due to the pattern of ascenders and descenders. The way to fix this is by using a *strut*, which is a zero-width box whose height and depth match the extremes of the font. If the keywords in your language are in lower case, say `\Strut` after the keyword in the terminal box — or, better yet, define a macro that does this, as in Appendix B. Struts are already included in nonterminal boxes, because these contain mostly lower-case letters.

Sometimes two rows would look better if they were moved a little bit closer together. You can do this by using `\TrimTop` or `\TrimBot`; these macros take an hlist as a parameter, box it, and then take a little off of the top or the bottom. Look at Appendix B to see how these can be used.

Appendix A and Appendix B

Editor's note:
Appendix A in the original paper was a six page listing of the `SynChart.TEX` file, and Appendix B was a ten page listing of a non-trivial example of the use of the syntax chart macros. These two appendices may be found as part of a scanned copy of the original paper at `http://tug.org/TUGboat/Articles/tb02-3/tb04plass.pdf`.

Page 52 of the original paper, the sixth page of Appendix B, also included the following editor's note:

> As you may have noticed [in the main text] of this paper, there are some problems with the font used to draw the quarter-circles. The paper copy Mike Plass sent in with his tape looks quite a bit better, and the remainder of his diagrams are reproduced from that copy, which was prepared on one of Xerox's printers.

Barbara Beeton remembers the situation as follows: the glitch in the joining of the lines and the quarter circles was a problem between the font and Michael's macros. The printer Michael used was a Xerox Dover at 384 dpi. The printer for the journal issues was an Alphatype CRS, with a resolution of 5333 dpi and output on large sheets of resin-coated photographic paper.

A scan follows of one of the figures in Appendix B.

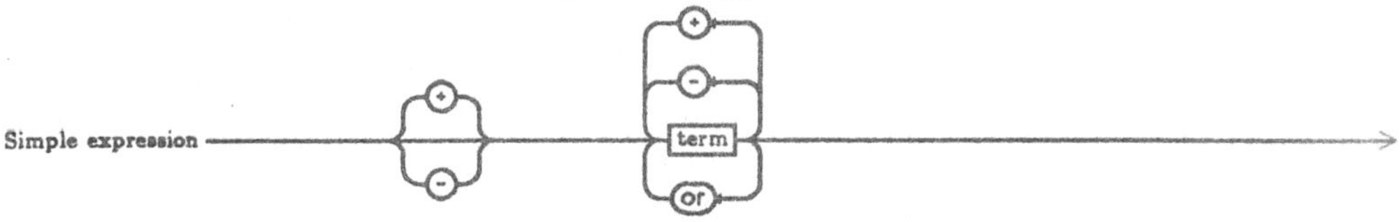

Long meeting with Mike [Plass] and Frank [Liang]
to discuss plan for TEX implementation.
Edited TEX.ONE draft
making various improvements to the language.

— DONALD KNUTH, *Diary entry* (1977)

One of the most challenging aspects of page layout
is the problem of breaking paragraphs of text into individual lines.
The fact that computers can do this task better
than all but the most dedicated hand-compositors
was one of my early motivations for developing the TEX system.

— DONALD KNUTH, *Digital Typography* (1999)

10

Tomas Rokicki

Tomas Rokicki was first introduced to TeX by Professor Norman Naugle in Tom's junior year at Texas A&M. At Texas A&M Tom wrote drivers to go from TeX to the then new QMS laser printers. Another task was to get TeX running on the school's Unix minicomputers; since the Unix Pascal compiler was not up to the task of compiling TeX, he wrote a script using `lex` and `yacc` to convert the TeX code to C. This was the genesis of the Web2c system used today to compile TeX.[1]

After attending an early TeX Users Group meeting at Stanford (ca. 1984) and meeting Donald Knuth, Barbara Beeton, David Fuchs, and others, and sensing the excitement in the computer science department, Tomas knew he wanted to attend graduate school at Stanford. During the summer of 1985, before his first term at Stanford, Tom began work on the TeX project, staying with David Fuchs while finding on-campus lodging. The primary work was the design and implementation of the PK tools. He wrote the tools to move in and out of the PK format and to do other things, enabling use of the PK format which reduced by half the storage required by the GF files.

Tom enjoyed his time at Stanford, learning from classes and classmates, including the CS 304 "Programming and Problem Solving Seminar" (featuring open-ended problems, as mentioned on page 67) which Tom both took and later TAed. Tom's PhD thesis was finished in 1993 and titled *Representing and Modeling Digital Circuits*.

A few years after arriving at Stanford, Tom began working on `dvips`, which he got working initially on the Amiga machine, around 1985–86. He improved and maintained `dvips` for a number of years, but over time a long list of other people made big improvements, including Donald Knuth.

After Stanford, Tom worked at HP until 1999 and then started Instantis with a few friends, where he continues to work. Tom lives in Palo Alto with his wife Sue and yellow Labrador Andy.

TUGboat bibliography

`Dvi_QMS`: An example of a driver	[**5**:2, November 1984]
`\special`	[**5**:2, November 1984]
Miscellaneous activity at Texas A&M (with Norman Naugle)	[**6**:2, July 1985]
Packed (PK) font file format	[**6**:3, November 1985]
TeX on the Amiga	[**7**:2, June 1986]
Packed file format update	[**7**:3, October 1986]
The Commodore Amiga: A magic TeX machine	[**9**:1, April 1988]
Advanced 'special' support in a DVI driver	[**15**:3, September 1994]
A proposed standard for specials	[**16**:4, December 1995]

[1] The content of this introduction is abstracted from Tom's TUG interview: `http://tug.org/interviews/rokicki.html`.

Packed (PK) font file format

[Published in *TUGboat* **6**:3, November 1985]

Pixel files, the output of METAFONT79, are now considered obsolete; their use is being discouraged. This is not surprising; as a font file format, they are rather limiting. They tend to be too large, do not include device character width information, and only allow 128 characters. Yet, the generic font file format offered in their place (with new METAFONT) has some other limitations. GF files tend to be almost as large as the pixel files they replace, and the character width data is separated from the raster data. A new format, called the packed, or PK format, is therefore being introduced.

This new file format is less than half the size of the GF format. Since input/output time usually dominates execution time when reading font files, the smaller size can also lead to a performance improvement. The new format is easier to interpret than the GF format. The minimum bounding box for the bitmaps is supplied; the horizontal and vertical size do not need to be checked against the actual bits of the character. The raster data and width data for each character are given in the same character 'packet'. Finally, the font parameters (checksum, design size, etc.) are given at the beginning of the font file, rather than at the end, so random file access is not needed.

An additional advantage is that the length of each character packet is given at the beginning of the packet. This means that the character packets can be directly stored into the memory of a driver without interpretation, and they can be interpreted on a demand basis. A recent sampling of font usage at Texas A&M University on their Electrical Engineering VAX showed that 18 characters per declared font were used on the average. Thus, a driver using the packed format might not need to interpret 110 of the 128 characters in a font, on the average.

The use of the packed file format does impose an extra step of processing between METAFONT and the driver, however. Also, the packed file format is based to a large extent on the four bit nybble rather than the eight bit byte, so individual bytes often need to be split as the file is being read in. In addition, the generic font format allows **specials** and **numspecial**s within character raster definitions; the packed file format does not. METAFONT never generates **special**s inside of character raster definitions, so this should not pose any problems.

The size improvement of packed files over pixel files is almost five to one for a large collection of fonts. 323 fonts at three hundred dots per inch and various magnifications were reduced by 79% when converted to the packed form. This makes the packed format ideal for microcomputer systems or any system where disk space is at a premium.

The packed file format is part of the METAFONTware, with which it will be distributed. Programs currently on the distribution are GFtoPK, which converts generic font files to packed files; PKtoPX, which converts packed files to pixel files: PXtoPK, which converts pixel files to packed files, and PKtype, which lists and verifies a packed file.

The rest of this article was extracted from PKtype, and is a full description of the packed file format.

1. Packed file format. The packed file format is a compact representation of the data contained in a GF file. The information content is the same, but packed (PK) files are almost always less than half the size of their GF counterparts. They are also easier to convert into a raster representation because they do not have a profusion of *paint*, *skip*, and *new_row* commands to be separately interpreted. In addition, the PK format expressly forbids **special** commands within a character. The minimum bounding box for each character is explicit in the format, and does not need to be scanned for as in the GF format. Finally, the width and escapement values are combined with the raster information into character 'packets', making it simpler in many cases to process a character.

A PK file is organized as a stream of 8-bit bytes. At times, these bytes might be split into 4-bit nybbles or single bits, or combined into multiple byte parameters. When bytes are split into smaller pieces, the 'first' piece is always the most significant of the byte. For instance, the first bit of a byte is the bit with value 128; the first nybble can be found by dividing a byte by 16. Similarly, when bytes are combined into multiple byte parameters, the first byte is the most significant of the parameter. If the parameter is signed, it is represented by two's-complement notation.

The set of possible eight-bit values is separated into two sets, those that introduce a character definition, and those that do not. The values that introduce a character definition comprise the range from 0 to 239; byte values above 239 are interpreted commands. Bytes which introduce character definitions are called flag bytes, and various fields within the byte indicate various things about how the character definition is encoded. Command bytes have zero or more parameters, and can never appear within a character definition or between parameters of another command, where they would be interpreted as data.

A PK file consists of a preamble, followed by a sequence of one or more character definitions, followed by a postamble. The preamble command must be the first byte in the file, followed immediately by its parameters. Any number of character definitions may follow, and any command but the preamble command and the postamble command may occur between character definitions. The very last command in the file must be the postamble.

2. The packed file format is intended to be easy to read and interpret by device drivers. The small size of the file reduces the input/output overhead each time a font is defined. For those drivers that load and save each font file into memory, the small size also helps reduce the memory requirements. The length of each character packet is specified, allowing the character raster data to be loaded into memory by simply counting bytes, rather than interpreting each command; then, each character can be interpreted on a demand basis. This also makes it possible for a driver to skip a particular character quickly if it knows that the character is unused.

3. First, the command bytes shall be presented; then the format of the Character definitions will be defined. Eight of the possible sixteen commands (values 240 through 255) are currently defined; the others are reserved for future extensions. The commands are listed below. Each command is specified by its symbolic name (e.g., *pk_no_op*), its opcode byte, and any parameters. The parameters are followed by a bracketed number telling how many bytes they occupy, with the number preceded by a plus sign if it is a signed quantity. (Four byte quantities are always signed, however.)

pk_xxx1 240 $k[1]$ $x[k]$. This command is undefined in general; it functions as a $(k+2)$-byte *no_op* unless special PK-reading programs are being used. METAFONT generates *xxx* commands when encountering a **special** string. It is recommended that x be a string having the form of a keyword followed by possible parameters relevant to that keyword.

pk_xxx2 241 $k[2]$ $x[k]$. Like *pk_xxx1*, but $0 \le k < 65536$.

pk_xxx3 242 $k[3]$ $x[k]$. Like *pk_xxx1*, but $0 \le k < 2^{24}$. METAFONT uses this when sending a special string whose length exceeds 255.

pk_xxx4 243 $k[4]$ $x[k]$. Like *pk_xxx1*, but k can be ridiculously large; k mustn't be negative.

pk_yyy 244 $y[4]$. This command is undefined in general; it functions as a five-byte *no_op* unless special PK reading programs are being used. METAFONT puts *scaled* numbers into *yyy*'s, as a result of **numspecial** commands; the intent is to provide numeric parameters to *xxx* commands that immediately precede.

pk_post 245. Beginning of the postamble. This command is followed by just enough *pk_no_op* commands to make the file a multiple of four bytes long; zero through three are usual, but four are also allowed. This should make the file easy to read on machines which pack four bytes to a word.

pk_no_op 246. No operation, do nothing. Any number of *pk_no_op*'s may appear between PK commands, but a *pk_no_op* cannot be inserted between a command and its parameters, between two parameters, or inside a character definition.

pk_pre 247 $i[1]$ $k[1]$ $x[k]$ $ds[4]$ $cs[4]$ $hppp[4]$ $vppp[4]$. Preamble command. Here, i is the identification byte of the file, currently equal to 89. The string x is merely a comment, usually indicating the source of the PK file. The parameters ds and cs are the design size of the file in $1/2^{16}$ points, and the checksum of the file, respectively. The checksum should match the TFM file and the GF files for this font. Parameters $hppp$ and $vppp$ are the ratios of pixels per point, horizontally and vertically, multiplied by 2^{16}; they can be used to correlate the font with specific device resolutions, magnifications, and 'at sizes'. Usually. the name of the PK file is formed by concatenating the font name (e.g., `amr10`) with the resolution at which the font is prepared in pixels per inch multiplied by the magnification factor, and the letters PK. For instance, amr10 at 300 dots per inch should be named `AMR10.300PK`; at one thousand dots per inch and magstephalf, it should be named `AMR10.1095PK`.

4. We put a few of the above opcodes into definitions for symbolic use by this program.

define $pk\_id = 89$ {the version of PK file described}
define $pk\_xxx1 = 240$ {**special** commands}
define $pk\_yyy = 244$ {**numspecial** commands}
define $pk\_post = 245$ {postamble}
define $pk\_no\_op = 246$ {no operation}
define $pk\_pre = 247$ {preamble}

5. The PK format has two conflicting goals; to pack character raster and size information as compactly as possible, while retaining ease of translation into raster and other forms. A suitable compromise was found in the use of run-encoding of the raster information. Instead of packing the individual bits of the character, we instead count the number of consecutive 'black' or 'white' pixels in a horizontal raster row, and then encode this number. Run counts are found for each row, from the top of the character to the bottom. This is essentially the way the GF format works. Instead of presenting each row individually, however, let us concatenate all of the horizontal raster rows into one long string of pixels, and encode this row. With knowledge of the width of the bit-map, the original character glyph can be easily reconstructed. In addition, we do not need special commands to mark the end of one row and the beginning of the next.

Next, let us put the burden of finding the minimum bounding box on the part of the font generator, since the characters will usually be used much more often than they are generated. The minimum bounding box is the smallest rectangle which encloses all 'black' pixels of a character. Let us also eliminate the need for a special end of character marker, by supplying exactly as many bits as are required to fill the minimum bounding box, from which the end of the character is implicit.

Let us next consider the distribution of the run counts. Analysis of several dozen pixel files at 300 dots per inch yields a distribution peaking at four, falling off slowly until ten, then a bit more steeply until twenty, and then asymptotically approaching the horizontal. Thus, the great majority of our run counts will fit in a four-bit nybble. The eight-bit byte is attractive for our run-counts, as it is the standard on many systems; however, the wasted four bits in the majority of cases seems a high price to pay. Another possibility is to use a Huffman-type encoding scheme with a variable number of bits for each run-count; this was rejected because of the overhead in fetching and examining individual bits in the file. Thus, the character raster definitions in the PK file format are based on the four bit nybble.

6. The analysis of the pixel files yielded another interesting statistic: fully 37% of the raster rows were duplicates of the previous row. Thus, the PK format allows the specification of repeat counts, which indicate how many times a horizontal raster row is to be repeated. These repeated rows are taken out of the character glyph before individual rows are concatenated into the long string of pixels.

For elegance, we disallow a run count of zero. The case of a null raster description should be gleaned from the character width and height being equal to zero, and no raster data should be read. No other zero counts are ever necessary. Also, in the absence of repeat counts, the repeat value is set to be zero (only the original row is sent). If a repeat count is seen, it takes effect on the current row. The current row is defined as the row on which the first pixel of the next run count will lie. The repeat count is set back to zero when the last pixel in the current row is seen, and the row is sent out.

This poses a problem for entirely black and entirely white rows, however. Let us say that the current row ends with four white pixels, and then we have five entirely empty rows, followed by a black pixel at the beginning of the next row, and the character width is ten pixels. We would like to use a repeat count, but there is no legal place to put it. If we put it before the white run count, it will apply to the current row. If we put it after, it applies to the row with the black pixel at the beginning. Thus, entirely white or entirely black repeated rows are always packed as large run counts (in this case, a white run count of 54) rather than repeat counts.

7. Now let us turn our attention to the actual packing of the run counts and repeat counts into nybbles. There are only sixteen possible nybble values. We need to indicate run counts and repeat counts. Since the run counts are much more common, we will devote the majority of the nybble values to them. We therefore indicate a repeat count by a nybble of 14 followed by a packed number, where a packed number will be explained later. Since the repeat count value of one is so common, we indicate a repeat one command by a single nybble of 15. A 14 followed by the packed number 1 is still legal for a repeat one count, however. The run counts are coded directly as packed numbers.

For packed numbers, therefore, we have the nybble values 0 through 13. We need to represent the positive integers up to, say, $2^{31}-1$. We would like the more common smaller numbers to take only one or two nybbles, and the infrequent large numbers to take three or more. We could therefore allocate one nybble value to indicate a large run count taking three or more nybbles. We do this with the value 0.

8. We are left with the values 1 through 13. We can allocate some of these, say *dyn_f*, to be one-nybble run counts. These will work for the run counts $1 \mathinner{..} dyn\_f$. For subsequent run counts, we will use a nybble greater than *dyn_f*, followed by a second nybble, whose value can run from 0 through 15. Thus, the two-byte nybble values will run from $dyn\_f + 1 \mathinner{..} (13 - dyn\_f) * 16 + dyn\_f$. We have our definition of large run count values now, being all counts greater than $(13 - dyn\_f) * 16 + dyn\_f$.

We can analyze our several dozen pixel files and determine an optimal value of *dyn_f*, and use this value for all of the characters. Unfortunately, values of *dyn_f* that pack small characters well tend to pack the large characters poorly, and values that pack large characters well are not efficient for the smaller characters. Thus, we choose the optimal *dyn_f* on a character basis, picking the value which will pack each individual character in the smallest number of nybbles. Legal values of *dyn_f* run from 0 (with no one-byte run counts) to 13 (with no two-byte run counts).

9. Our only remaining task in the coding of packed numbers is the large run counts. We use a scheme suggested by D. E. Knuth which will simply and elegantly represent arbitrarily large values. The general scheme to represent an integer i is to write its hexadecimal representation, with leading zeros removed. Then we count the number of digits, and prepend one less than that many zeros before the hexadecimal representation. Thus, the values from one to fifteen occupy one nybble; the values sixteen through 255 occupy three, the values 256 through 4095 require five, etc.

For our purposes, however, we have already represented the numbers one through $(13 - dyn\_f) * 16 + dyn\_f$. In addition, the one-nybble values have already been taken by our other commands, which means that only the values from sixteen up are available to us for long run counts. Thus, we simply normalize our long run counts, by subtracting $(13 - dyn\_f) * 16 + dyn\_f + 1$ and adding 16, and then representing the result according to the scheme above.

10. The final algorithm for decoding the run counts based on the above scheme might look like this, assuming a procedure called *pk_nyb* is available to get the next nybble from the file, and assuming that the global *repeat_count* indicates whether a row needs to be repeated. Note that this routine is recursive, but since a repeat count can never directly follow another repeat, count, it can only be recursive to one level. [The algorithm shown here is the final one from `pktype.web`, rather than the one printed in the original article. — *Ed.*]

```
function pk_packed_num: integer;
 var i, j: integer;
 begin i ← get_nyb;
 if i = 0 then
    begin repeat j ← get_nyb; incr(i);
    until j ≠ 0;
    while i > 0 do
       begin j ← j * 16 + get_nyb; decr(i);
```

```
        end;
      pk_packed_num ← j − 15 + (13 − dyn_f) * 16 + dyn_f;
      end
   else if i ≤ dyn_f then pk_packed_num ← i
      else if i < 14 then pk_packed_num ← (i − dyn_f − 1) * 16 + get_nyb + dyn_f + 1
        else begin if repeat_count ≠ 0 then
              abort('Second␣repeat␣count␣for␣this␣row!');
          repeat_count ← 1;  { prevent recursion more than one level }
          if i = 14 then repeat_count ← pk_packed_num;
          send_out(true, repeat_count);
          pk_packed_num ← pk_packed_num;
          end;
   end;
```

11. For low resolution fonts, or characters with 'gray' areas, run encoding can often make the character many times larger. Therefore, for those characters that cannot be encoded efficiently with run counts, the PK format allows bit-mapping of the characters. This is indicated by a *dyn_f* value of 14. The bits are packed tightly, by concatenating all of the horizontal raster rows into one long string, and then packing this string eight bits to a byte. The number of bytes required can be calculated by $(width * height + 7)$ **div** 8. This format should only be used when packing the character by run counts takes more bytes than this, although, of course, it is legal for any character. Any extra bits in the last byte should be set to zero.

12. At this point, we are ready to introduce the format for a character descriptor. It consists of three parts: a flag byte, a character preamble, and the raster data. The most significant four nybbles of the flag byte yield the *dyn_f* value for that character. (Notice that only values of 0 through 14 are legal for *dyn_f*, with 14 indicating a bit mapped character; thus, the flag bytes do not conflict with the command bytes, whose upper nybble is always 15.) The next bit (with weight 16) indicates whether the first run count is a black count or a white count, with a one indicating a black count. For bit-mapped characters, this bit should be set to a zero. The next bit (with weight 8) indicates whether certain later parameters (referred to as size parameters) are given in one-byte or two-byte quantities, with a one indicating that they are in two-byte quantities. The last two bits are concatenated on to the beginning of the length parameter in the character preamble, which will be explained below.

However, if the last three bits of the flag byte are all set (normally indicating that the size parameters are two-byte values and that a 3 should be prepended to the length parameter), then a long format of the character preamble should be used instead of one of the short forms.

Therefore, there are three formats for the character preamble, and which one is used depends on the least significant three bits of the flag byte. If the least significant three bits are in the range zero through three, the short format is used. If they are in the range four through six, the extended short format is used. Otherwise, if the least significant bits are all set, then the long form of the character preamble is used. The preamble formats are explained below.

Short form: *flag*[1] *pl*[1] *cc*[1] *tfm*[3] *dm*[1] *w*[1] *h*[1] *hoff*[+1] *voff*[+1]. If this format of the character preamble is used, the above parameters must all fit in the indicated number of bytes, signed or unsigned as indicated. Almost all of the standard TEX font characters fit; the few exceptions are huge fonts such as `aminch`.

Extended short form: *flag*[1] *pl*[2] *cc*[1] *tfm*[3] *dm*[2] *w*[2] *h*[2] *hoff*[+2] *voff*[+2]. Larger characters use this extended format.

Long form: *flag*[1] *pl*[4] *cc*[4] *tfm*[4] *dx*[4] *dy*[4] *w*[4] *h*[4] *hoff*[4] *voff*[4]. This is the general format which allows all of the parameters of the GF file format, including vertical escapement.

The *flag* parameter is the flag byte. The parameter *pl* (packet length) contains the offset of the byte following this character descriptor, with respect to the beginning of the *tfm* width parameter. This is given so a PK reading program can, once it has read the flag byte, packet length, and character code (*cc*), skip over the character by simply reading this many more bytes. For the two short forms of the character preamble, the last two bits of the flag byte should be considered the two most-significant bits of the packet length. For the short format, the true packet length might be calculated as $(\mathit{flag} \mathbin{\mathbf{mod}} 4) * 256 + pl$; for the extended format, it might be calculated as $(\mathit{flag} \mathbin{\mathbf{mod}} 4) * 65536 + pl$.

The *w* parameter is the width and the *h* parameter is the height in pixels of the minimum bounding box. The *dx* and *dy* parameters are the horizontal and vertical escapements, respectively. In the short formats, *dy* is assumed to be zero and *dm* is *dy* but in pixels; in the long format, *dx* and *dy* are both in pixels multiplied by 2^{16}. The *hoff* is the horizontal offset from the upper left pixel to the reference pixel; the *voff* is the vertical offset. They are both given in pixels, with right and down being positive. The reference pixel is the pixel which occupies the unit square in METAFONT; the METAFONT reference point is the lower left hand corner of this pixel. (See the example below.)

13. TEX requires that all characters which have the same character codes modulo 256 also have the same *tfm* widths, and escapement values. The PK format does not itself make this a requirement, but in order for the font to work correctly with the TEX software, this constraint should be observed. The current version of TEX (1.5) cannot output character codes greater than 255 anyway.

Following the character preamble is the raster information for the character, packed by run counts or by bits, as indicated by the flag byte. If the character is packed by run counts and the required number of nybbles is odd, then the last byte of the raster description should have a zero for its least significant nybble.

14. As an illustration of the PK format, the character Ξ from the font amr10 at 300 dots per inch will be encoded. This character was chosen because it illustrates some of the borderline cases. The raster for the character looks like this (the row numbers are chosen for convenience, and are not METAFONT's row numbers.)

```
 0    MMMMMMMMMMMMMMMMMMMM
 1    MMMMMMMMMMMMMMMMMMMM
 2    MMMMMMMMMMMMMMMMMMMM
 3    MMMMMMMMMMMMMMMMMMMM
 4    MM                MM
 5    MM                MM
 6    MM                MM
 7
 8
 9      MM            MM
10      MM            MM
11      MM            MM
12      MMMMMMMMMMMMMMMM
13      MMMMMMMMMMMMMMMM
```

```
14       MMMMMMMMMMMMMMMM
15       MMMMMMMMMMMMMMMM
16       MM            MM
17       MM            MM
18       MM            MM
19
20
21
22     MM                MM
23     MM                MM
24     MM                MM
25     MMMMMMMMMMMMMMMMMMMM
26     MMMMMMMMMMMMMMMMMMMM
27     MMMMMMMMMMMMMMMMMMMM
28  *  MMMMMMMMMMMMMMMMMMMM
```

The width of the minimum bounding box for this character is 20; its height is 29. The '*' represents the reference pixel; notice how it lies outside the minimum bounding box. The *hoff* value is -2, and the *voff* is 28.

The first task is to calculate the run counts and repeat counts. The repeat counts are placed at the first transition (black to white or white to black) in a row, and are enclosed in brackets. White counts are enclosed in parentheses. It is relatively easy to generate the counts list:

82 [2] (16) 2 (42) [2] 2 (12) 2 (4) [3] 16 (4) [2] 2 (12) 2 (62) [2] 2 (16) 82

Note that any duplicated rows that are not all white or all black are removed before the repeat counts are calculated. The rows thus removed are rows 5, 6, 10, 11, 13, 14, 15, 17, 18, 23, and 24.

15. The next step in the encoding of this character is to calculate the optimal value of *dyn_f*. The details of how this calculation is done are not important here; suffice it to say that there is a simple algorithm which in one pass over the count list can determine the best value of *dyn_f*. For this character, the optimal value turns out to be 8 (atypically low). Thus, all count values less than or equal to 8 are packed in one nybble; those from nine to $(13-8)*16+8$ or 88 are packed in two nybbles. The run encoded values now become (in hex, separated according to the above list):

```
D9 E2 97 2 B1 E2 2 93 2 4 E3
97 4 E2 2 93 2 C5 E2 2 97 D9
```

which comes to 36 nybbles, or 18 bytes. This is shorter than the 73 bytes required for the bit map, so we use the run count packing.

16. The short form of the character preamble is used because all of the parameters fit in their respective lengths. The packet length is therefore 18 bytes for the raster, plus eight bytes for the character preamble parameters following the character code, or 26. The *tfm* width for this character is 640796, or `9C71C` in hexadecimal. The horizontal escapement is 25 pixels. The flag byte is 88 hex, indicating the short preamble, the black first count, and the *dyn_f* value of 8. The final total character packet, in hexadecimal, is:

Flag byte	`88`
Packet length	`1A`
Character code	`04`
tfm width	`09 C7 1C`
Horizontal escapement (pixels)	`19`
Width of bit map	`14`
Height of bit map	`1D`
Horizontal offset (signed)	`FE`
Vertical offset	`1C`
Raster data	`D9 E2 97`
	`2B 1E 22`
	`93 24 E3`
	`97 4E 22`
	`93 2C 5E`
	`22 97 D9`

PK was announced to the world by Tom Rokicki (student of Knuth and developer of dvips) in 1985. PK solves the main problems of the GF format: its complexity and its size.

— YANNIS HARALAMBOUS, *Fonts & Encodings* (2007)

TUG
2000

11
Luis Trabb Pardo

Luis Trabb Pardo is originally from Argentina, where he taught at the University of Buenos Aires before going, in 1973, to Stanford to study for a Ph.D. in computer science. Donald Knuth was his advisor. Luis thinks perhaps his 1978 thesis, *Set Representation and Set Intersection*, was the last typewritten one at Stanford's CS department.

During his student years at Stanford, Luis also co-wrote a paper with Knuth entitled "The Early Development of Programming Languages," which included an simple algorithm used to compare various programming languages. This algorithm has become well known as the Trabb Pardo–Knuth algorithm.

After finishing his PhD, Luis stayed working for Knuth, helping out with TEX in the years 1978–1981. Luis recalls having some rather fancy title, e.g., "Associate Director, TEX Project." He helped mostly by working with people that were getting TEX and looking into what could be done to print document proofs. They interfaced to Varian and Versatec electrostatic plotters and Luis himself developed an interface for a prototype LBP-10 laser printer. Luis was also a reader for the PhD theses of both Michael Plass and Frank Liang, who both had Knuth as their thesis supervisor.

Eventually, Luis left Stanford and co-founded Imagen Corporation, which built controllers and printers. TEX and troff were used to drive these printers. Later, desktop publishing was added to their product mix.

Since Imagen, Luis has worked mostly on technology and architectures for very fast printing, including starting three small companies: The Aurora Group I, II and III.

TUGboat bibliography: The paper included here is Luis's only item in *TUGboat.*

The status of the PASCAL implementation of TEX

[Published in *TUGboat* **1**:1, October 1980]

[*Co-authored with Ignacio Zabala, dated September 9, 1980.*]

This document (`PTEX.TXT[TEX,IAZ]%SAIL`) is intended as a public, up-to-date report on the status of the PASCAL implementation of TEX. A file `PTEX.BBD[TEX,IAZ]%SAIL` is maintained that contains all the mail and new events related to PTEX.

System organization

The TEX-PASCAL system consists mainly of three modules:

- the TEXPRE module implements the pre-processor that generates the data structures employed by TEX.
- the SYSDEP module contains routines that are very much dependent on the particular host system. It is used both by TEXPRE and TEX.
- the main TEX module.

Compatibilities and uncompatibilities

Neither TEX nor TEXPRE should need modification at any installation, but, surely, SYSDEP must be adjusted for each host site. The three modules are programmed in PASCAL though some installations may find it convenient to reprogram SYSDEP in assembler language for the rake of execution speed.

As the default case in the CASE statement is a non-standard feature of PASCAL, it has been given different names by different compilers. Compile time initialization is not standard either, but available under different names in most compilers. These are the only reasons why TEX and TEXPRE may have to be modified, and the modifications are straightforward.

PTEX Installation

TEX-PASCAL has been running in the PDP-10 (SAIL) machine in our CS Dept., here at Stanford, since April 1980. Since then, all changes made by Don Knuth in the SAIL program have been incorporated immediately into the PASCAL program, which has also undergone modifications as more information was obtained on the characteristics of widely used PASCAL compilers. The program has been in-house tested. It has already processed the whole TEX manual and several chapters of Knuth's *Art of Computer Programming*.

Stanford's CIT has an IBM machine of the 370 family. Eagle Berns is in charge of the installation of TEX there. He has obtained a copy of the new IBM PASCAL VS compiler, and has tried to compile PTEX with it. As of September 9, both TEXPRE and SYSDEP (in PASCAL, only slightly modified) had compiled and run successfully to generate the table of data structures employed by the main TEX module. For these trials, Berns used 36 bpw font information files from SAIL. There was a problem with two procedures in the main TEX module which were still too large for the VS compiler. This module has been modified accordingly and we are waiting for feedback from Berns.

Charles Lawson is installing PTEX on the UNIVAC 1100 of the Jet Propulsion Lab at Caltech using the University of Wisconsin PASCAL compiler. He has made a good programming effort to get PTEX up. (For instance, he has coded the "environment" modules required by his compiler.) This installation seems to be already past the compilation phase.

At the University of Minnesota, Mike Frisch is installing PTEX on a CDC-Cyber.

George Otto is in charge of the installation at Wharton. The Moore school has a UWAC 90-VS/9 where they use the PASCAL-8000 compiler.

David Kashtan has compiled everything successfully on the VAX (VMS) at SRI.

Richard Friday has also compiled everything on a VAX (UNIX) at DEC.

TEX-PASCAL has been distributed to more centers: Stanford Linear Accelerator Center, University of Aarhus in Denmark, Universities of Milan and Pisa in Italy, University of Valencia in Spain, etc. The ones mentioned above have given the most feedback.

At this time, it seems that most pioneer installations are free of compilation problems and are now trying to obtain adequately interfaced output devices, together with fonts and font information files suitable for them.

The only fully operational PTEX system is still this at Stanford CSD, but we expect to be printing DVI files produced by the CIT installation very soon.

Compiler issues

TEX-PASCAL was developed using the Hamburg PASCAL compiler for the PDP-10 by Kisicki and Nagel. Some compiler maintenance was needed during the debugging of PTEX. We have found this to be a rather powerful and permissive compiler.

There have only been three system requirements on PTEX hosts and these were explicit since the beginning of the project:

- The system must have enough addressable memory to store the large arrays employed by PTEX (about 128K words of 32 bits).
- The compiler should be able to really pack fields of a PACKED RECORD and overlap multiple variants of packed records. If this requisite is not satisfied, PTEX will require at least four times as much memory.
- The compiler should be able to handle large case statements (say over 64 actual cases in a range $[-500\,..\,500]$) and have a default case (this is non-standard in PASCAL but available in most compilers).

Additionally, PTEX requires an EXTERNAL (or separate) compilation facility. If no such thing is available, the SYSDEP module has to be inserted both in TEX and in TEXPRE by hand. Also, if there is no compile time variable initialization, the INITPROCEDURE appearing in the program has to be changed into an ordinary procedure.

We have fought not to add more requirements and have changed the program to facilitate the installation with simpler or more restrictive compilers. Encountered problems have been common to most pioneer installations:

- lines of code are too long
- octal constants were not accepted
- identifiers containing the underscore character were not accepted
- some identifiers were too long
- sometimes two different identifiers were equal in the first eight characters
- fields of packed records could not be passed as procedure arguments
- loop counters had to be local variables
- all declared labels had to be used
- use of GOTOs was restricted: not even allowed from the body of a procedure

out to the block in which the procedure was declared

- there were discrepancies in the treatment of nested WITH statements
- the compiler lacked the standard MAX and MIN functions
- procedures had to be kept small (less than 400 statements)

The program has been modified to avoid them. Currently, the code is all uppercase in lines that are never longer than 72 characters. All identifiers are shorter than 16 characters and differ in the first 8 characters. Octal variables appear only in SYSDEP.

Distributions

Currently, TEX-PASCAL can be obtained from the TEX group at the CS Dept. at Stanford. Anyone asking for the system will get a tape containing the files `TEX.PAS`, `TEXPRE.PAS`, `SYSDEP.PAS`, `TEX.STR`, `TEXPRE.STR`, and `SYSDEP.STR`, which is about everything that is needed to have PTEX running. The distribution package also contains a short installation guide, a description of the DVI format of the output file of TEX, and extensively documented listings of TEX, TEXPRE and SYSDEP. (Of course, the ultimate documentation on TEX is the TEX manual.) All these files (not the listings) are available on-line in the directory `(TEX.PASCAL)%SCORE`, accessible via the `ARPANET`.

Fonts and font information files may also be provided on request (in the format employed here at SAIL). These files are very system-and-output-device-dependent and of restricted general value for that reason.

Luis Trabb Pardo and David R. Fuchs were my "right-hand men" for TEX78 and TEX82, respectively.

— DONALD KNUTH, *Software — Practice and Experience* (1989)

Luis Trabb Pardo and Ignacio Zabala subsequently used DOC to prepare a highly portable version of TEX in PASCAL, completed in April of 1980.

— DONALD KNUTH, *Software — Practice and Experience* (1989)

We had a student at Stanford whose name was Zabala. He took the entire TEX that I'd written in a language called SAIL, and converted it to Pascal . . .

— DONALD KNUTH, *Prague Q&A session* (1996)

edutex

12
Howard Trickey

Howard Trickey grew up in Toronto and started programming (in 1972) in high school. He attended the University of Toronto, taking an undergraduate degree in engineering science, while continuing to take every opportunity to program for fun. He also enjoyed using a computer for document preparation and used the IBM/360 ATS system for for mechanizing engineering documentation with lineprinter output for his bachelor's thesis.

Howard did a masters thesis at the University of Toronto, on parsing, using Unix and troff to typeset it.

In 1980 Howard moved to Stanford for a PhD in computer science. Even before heading off, He remembers buying and reading *TEX: a system for technical text* describing TEX 78 even before heading for Stanford.

At Stanford my thesis advisor was Jeff Ullman and his thesis topic was silicon compilation, however he continued to do programming for fun and typesetting. Donald Knuth was in the middle of a rewrite of the TEX program from Sail into Pascal, and he was taking the opportunity to update the language some as well. Knuth was using a big DEC machine running the Stanford SAIL operating system. Howard really wanted to run TEX, but on Unix, and Knuth's code did not compile on Unix, for reasons explained in the following paper. Howard did necessary modifications to the compiler and to operating system calls, resulting in TEX on Unix. Later Howard joined forces with Pavel Curtis at Cornell (who also did a port to Unix), and they maintainers of the Unix TEX changefile until the web2c approach obsoleted their efforts.

Howard also typically attended an informal weekly meeting where he talked about his progress on TEX.[1] He also at one point served as teaching assistant for an advanced algorithms course taught by Knuth.

Nearer to the end of Howard's five years at Stanford, LATEX needed a bibliography system and Oren Patashnik was working on BibTEX. Howard helped by writing the first four BibTEX styles.

From Stanford Howard went to AT&T Bell Labs Research (which later became Lucent Bell Labs Research), where he worked on a range of computer research projects, including graph drawing, operating systems, compilers, databases, wireless optimization, and software quality. During the first couple of years at Bell Labs, he brought the laboratory in which he worked TEX world by making dvi drivers for the various printers they had. For fun he ported TeX to a Cray that they had. After 20 years at Bell Labs, Howard moved to Google's New York office, where he has been working on Google Maps, first as a programmer and later as a manager.

TUGboat bibliography: The paper included here is Howard's only item in *TUGboat*.

[1] Oren Patashnik has mentioned Joe Weening and Frank Yellin also attending these informal sessions.

Porting TeX to VAX/UNIX

[Published in *TUGboat* **4**:1, April 1983]

[*Co-authored with Pavel Curtis.*]

Over the past few months, the authors have independently ported TeX82 to run under Berkeley's VAX/Unix[2] (version 4.1BSD). One of us (Pavel) subsequently merged our ideas to produce the VAX/Unix distribution of TeX announced in this issue's Unix TeX Site Report. Both implementations required small changes to Berkeley's *pc* compiler. This note describes the problems encountered in making these changes and in bringing up TeX itself.

TeX porters are aware that the capabilities of the available Pascal compiler will almost totally determine how difficult the port will be. Unhappily, the *pc* compiler has more deficiencies than one might wish. This is somewhat understandable, since it was designed for instructional use and not for the preparation of production software. On the plus side, the documentation was good enough to allow us to anticipate most of the problems. Also, we seem to be the exception to "Fuchs' Law" that TeX uncovers at least one compiler bug for every compiler tried—our problems were caused by deficiencies, not bugs. This meant that there were few unexpected problems, and we were able to do the initial port in surprisingly little time (one or two weeks).

The *most* significant shortcoming of *pc* was also the one major place where Professor Knuth departed from Jensen and Wirth's Pascal and from the proposed standard: a default clause in the **case** statement. It has been suggested that the best way to handle this problem is to write a program to translate the **case** statements used in TeX to **case** statements without default clauses. This is actually fairly difficult to do properly, since it entails discovering the type of the case expression (character, integer, or integer subrange) and then forming a succinct test for the gaps between the expressions that actually occur as case labels. Since the *pc* compiler already generates code to check for an unmentioned value, the best possible translation would result in doing this work twice. The old PTeX implementation made a half-hearted attempt, by using an editor script to collect most of the information needed, but one still had to do the translation manually. We considered it imperative that bringing up a new version of TeX be fast and easy, enabling all installations to track bug fixes and added features.

The last thing one normally resorts to in order to circumvent a language deficiency is that horror of horrors: compiler modification. No one except the author or maintainer of a compiler really understands the implications of a given change to the code, so it is easy to introduce obscure bugs. Also, the compiler modifier has to be wary of new versions of the compiler from its maintainer. Having said this, we must now say that we both came to the conclusion, in this case, that compiler modification was the answer. Examination of the then current code showed that *pc* was already trapping the default case in order to have an error message printed. It was immediately obvious how to give control to another statement instead, and it was hard to see how any bugs could be introduced. Since so few changes were needed, the new-compiler-version problem was not too daunting, so the deed was done.

Compiler modification was definitely not the answer for the next problem, memory packing. To avoid wasting a large amount of memory, we needed to define the types

[2]Unix and VAX are registered trademarks of Bell Laboratories and Digital Equipment Corporation.

quarterword and *halfword* to contain 8 and 16 bits, respectively. It is not possible to convince *pc* to pack 0..65535 into 16 bits or 0..255 into 8 bits. While it might not be too difficult to get the memory allocator to do this, the code generator could easily be a different question. Fortunately, the compiler *will* pack −128..127 and −32768..32767 into the proper sizes and TeX has been written so that these ranges can be easily used in the all important *memory_word* record. A similar problem occurs with the non-character *byte_files*, but here one must be careful that the bits actually written to the files look like the range 0..255 has been used (otherwise, device independent output files and TeX font metric files can't be transported between sites). So, for example, instead of writing a value of 200 to a file, we write 200 − 256 = −56.

In spite of the above, we would still waste a tremendous amount of memory if we could not find a way to fit the type called *glue_ratio* into 32 bits. Usually a *glue-ratio* is made the same as **real**, but *pc* puts **reals** into 64 bits, and has no provision for any kind of "short" **reals**. Fortunately, the VAX hardware has a 32-bit floating point data type, so the following trick could be used: Pascal is told that a **glue-ratio** is a (32-bit) integer, but we really store floating point numbers there; external procedures (written in C) are then used to convert back and forth between those pseudo-**reals** and *pc*'s 64-bit variety.

The rest of the changes necessary were more conventional. There were a few places where TeX uses variables names that *pc* uses for special things (e.g., *input*, *text*, *time*, and *date*), but the `WEB` system provided an easy way to fix them. The *pc* runtime system doesn't provide for recovery from file opening errors, or for closing a file immediately. It was easy to modify a few of the run-time library procedures to make files behave the way TeX assumes they will. Specifically, the following changes were made:

- Opening an input or output file that isn't there causes the "end-of-file" flag to be set true or false, respectively, rather than being a fatal error.
- Reading past end-of-file is silently ignored, rather than being a fatal error.
- The first **get** from the terminal is now ignored.
- Provision is made to explicitly close a file. The *pc* run-time system as supplied simply closes files on scope exit.

The alternative to changing the run-time library would be to do all input/output with external C procedures, but this would have meant changing every place in the code that used **get**, **put**, **read**, **write**, tests for end-of-fie, etc. Macros would have helped to some extent, but it is hard to see how to convert a file variable argument into information that conveys the type of the file. Also, one has to be on guard for a varying number of arguments. Adding onto this the need to simulate Pascal's conventions about text files, it just seemed easier to make the run-time library changes.

One particularly irritating thing about *pc* is that it doesn't accept keywords which are written using uppercase characters, even though that is required by the standard! (More precisely, there is a flag allowing for upper case keywords to be used but this switch also turns off all of the other extensions Berkeley *did* make to the Jensen and Wirth standard.) There were a number of places in `TANGLE` that had to be changed in order to prevent the conversion to uppercase. A subtle bug can show up if one is not careful in making this change: when `TANGLE` does constant folding, it looks for keywords like `MOD` and `DIV` in the output buffer. The easiest place to convert to lowercase is before these comparisons, and if the comparisons are not changed an incorrect program may result.

Another problem we had with TANGLE was getting it to put the statement

```
#include "ext.h"
```

in the Pascal output. This statement is needed to tell *pc* about externally compiled procedures. The double quote marks in the statement could not be emitted by TANGLE, and there was no way to force the '#' to be just after a line break. We introduced primitives into WEB that eventually evolved into the "verbatim Pascal string" and the "force Pascal line break" primitives now in the standard WEB language.

The amount of time it takes to compile is a major annoyance. Using an otherwise unloaded VAX 11/780, it takes approximately an hour of real time to create a runnable TEX from the WEB source code. Back in the real world, one of us has experienced upwards of a five hour wait when other people were using the machine. Now that the port is complete, this is no longer such a bother. On those infrequent occasions when a new version of TEX is being installed, one can simply have the compilation done in the middle of the night.

For regular use, it appears necessary to have a version of the program which has the PLAIN macros preloaded. Unfortunately, UNIX is not as amenable to this idea as some other systems, notably TOPS-20. We were able, however, to retrieve a program from the net.sources group on USENET which will do the trick. The program, called "undump", takes a core-image and the executable file which produced it and constructs a new executable file incorporating all of the data areas of the core-image. After some involved machinations and close perusal of the order of file opens or closes within TEX, a procedure was derived for preloading any macro set. This saves an average of 30 seconds or so of start-up time over the non-preloaded version.

Some statistics regarding the port are in order. The production version compiles into about 235,000 bytes of code. This doesn't include the large data arrays, which need not be allocated until runtime. At least 250,000 bytes of data area are needed in addition to the code to get a usable TEX. In a memory-rich system it is not unreasonable to allocate 500,000 bytes for this purpose. It is possible, as mentioned above, to save a version of TEX that has its data areas preloaded with fonts and macros, but one wouldn't want to have too many such versions; they are on the order of 750,000 bytes long each. As for running speed, a sample six-page paper (single-spaced, 10-point type, using a page of macros and a couple of fonts on top of PLAIN) took 44 cpu seconds to format using the preloaded-with-PLAIN version of the program. For comparison, the same paper took 37 cpu seconds on the SAIL DEC-10 computer used to develop TEX.

With regard to output drivers for UNIX, there are not many yet available. One of us (Howard) has a driver written in C for the Xerox Dover printer "press" format, adapted from a program that handled the old (version 1) DVI files. The new program handles either version. Pavel has written one for the Imagen/Canon Imprint Laser Printer, also in C.

Looking back on the port, it must be said that the combination of the WEB system and Professor Knuth's careful coding has resulted in quite a portable program. It now takes less than a day to bring up a new version of TEX and check that it passes the nefarious TRIP test. It is rarely necessary to touch the changes we've made, since the new features and bug fixes usually don't occur in the "system-dependent" parts. As a result, TEX is a program that can easily stay up to date and incorporate the latest bug fixes at many sites on many hosts. That, combined with the care taken to ensure that the output will be the exactly the same from host to host, means that we have a solid basis for portable documents.

The largest change was the release of TeX, Version 1.0,
on December 10, 1983. At that time,
Howard Trickey also provided new versions of Tangle and Weave
that replaced the [PASCAL] input statements with C language routines
and we all marveled at the resulting speedup.

— RICHARD FURUTA, *TUGboat Unix Site Report* (1984)

Sometime between 1990 and 1995,
TEX captured the mathematical world completely.
It was a revolution.

— DICK KOCH, *TUG Interviews* (2007)
http://tug.org/interviews

The current era seems to be one of great stability:
TEX and LATEX itself are now firmly settled with refinements to packages ...,
ever-improving installation via the TEX Live CDs, better package documentation ...

— CHRISTINA THIELE, *TUG Interviews* (2007)

Between the easy distribution of packages through CTAN
and a better process in LATEX 2_ε for integrating packages,
the number of packages seems to have exploded.
It is also easier to find and distribute documentation,
so there is a lot better process for finding out how to do things.

— DAN LUECKING, *TUG Interviews* (2004)

(LA)TEX books
are useful to people in virtually every scientific and technical discipline,
and they are so throughout the world
(one reader we heard from was a urologist in Kenya).

— PETER GORDON, *TUG Interviews* (2008)

One of the main reasons I recommend LATEX is I often meet grad students
who are groaning about the pain of dealing with their bibliographies
A user of LATEX/BIBTEX who has a sensible Makefile never has any such pain.
The bibliography just happens,
and is perfectly formatted in whatever house style is desired.

— DAVID MACKAY, *TUG Interviews* (2009)

... if we are over-zealous in respecting Don's wish that TEX remain unchanged
(modulo essential bug-fixes made by himself)
for perpetuity, we will end up with a museum piece
rather than an archetype of leading-edge technology.

— PHILIP TAYLOR, *TUG Interviews* (2005)

... there are so many developments:
modern TEXs don't have the arbitrary restrictions of the original programs,
we can now produce a beautiful web-friendly PDF with ease,
we are seeing solutions to the font issues that frustrate even reasonably skilled users,
and people are developing for the future ...

— JIM HEFFERON, *TUG Interviews* (2007)

www.ingramcontent.com/pod-product-compliance
Ingram Content Group UK Ltd.
Pitfield, Milton Keynes, MK11 3LW, UK
UKHW052228270726
14060UKWH00004B/660

9 780982 462614